#200

To Betty
From

La Vada

Prayer
in the Market Place

a collection from
Good Business

UNITY SCHOOL OF CHRISTIANITY
LEE'S SUMMIT, MO.
1959

Prayer in the Market Place
was first published in 1950.
This is the third printing.

This is one of a series of Unity books devoted
to teaching how you can make your life better by
applying Christian principles. The first Unity
book, *Lessons in Truth,* was published in 1894
and is still in publication. The Unity work itself
was established in 1889, when its founders,
Charles and Myrtle Fillmore, began to share with
others the Truth that had helped them.

The Unity movement now reaches millions of
persons all over the world. Unity School of Christianity includes the Silent Unity department, to
which thousands of people each year write for
prayers for any need, and the Publishing Department, which distributes the Unity books and magazines that carry the Unity message around the
world. Unity centers and churches are located in
many large cities.

Foreword

One day long ago, money-changers were angry because a man drove them from the temple. His belief was that they should not take their business into the temple but should take the temple into their business. Time has proved the man right, so now the money-changers (all the people engaged in the business of making a living) are increasingly adopting His principles as the best basis for success. This book sets forth the principles and tells how modern people are applying them with increasing satisfaction. The material in the book has been tested, also, for it is composed of the most popular articles that have appeared in *Good Business* magazine—as judged by the readers.

CONTENTS

Prayer in the Market Place

Prayer in the Market Place

CLARENCE EDWIN FLYNN

Bless Thou that which I purchase;
  Bless Thou that which I sell.
Bless Thou my daily labor;
  Help me to do it well.
Bless Thou my chosen mission;
  Upon it set Thy seal.
Bless those who work beside me;
  Bless those with whom I deal.

Bless Thou my place of service;
  Bless Thou the plans I cast;
Bless Thou the means that bring them
  To form and life at last.
Bless roads my works may travel,
  Each place they come to rest,
Each one whose life they strengthen:
  Then I too shall be blessed.

It Didn't Just Happen

GARDNER HUNTING

Y EARS AGO Western Union delivered its messages in special envelopes. A thin wire was threaded through the envelope so that you could slip a thumbnail under a narrow loop of it and rip the envelope open by a pull. It worked, sometimes, when you could find the loop.

But once at least it worked remarkably for me. My brother, who was perhaps sixteen then, was a Western Union messenger. One day he attempted to deliver a message at a house where he found nobody at home. So he brought the message back to the office and set it up on the operator's desk. (There was only one operator in that small town office.) My brother was a careful messenger, so he put the envelope, with its little ripping-wire, carefully where it would get attention. He put it across a pair of telegraph instruments, where it would stand up in plain sight of all concerned.

Now it "happens" that electric current will always follow the line of least resistance. A message presently came in over one outside wire to one of the keys where that wired envelope rested. What happened? You can guess faster than I can write it. The message was transferred from one key to the

other on which the wired envelope rested, by means
of that line of least resistance that was the ripping-
wire in the envelope. The message crossed the gap
between the keys and went out on the second wire.

Of course it caused a little confusion, but no harm
was done. Nobody got much excited about it when
the mistake was discovered and corrected—that is,
nobody but *me!* It "happened" that I was trying
to write stories, and getting no returns but rejection
slips. When my brother told me about the little incident in the telegraph office, I saw a story in it. It
"happened" that a magazine was offering prizes for
short stories, ranging from a first prize of five thousand dollars down to about a twenty-fifth prize of
fifty dollars. I thought it would be nice to win one
of those prizes; so I wrote my patent-envelope story
and sent it off, hoping.

This is a story of coincidences, which "happen"
every day but are ruled out of fiction stories by editors who say they are unbelievable. It "happened"
that I, living in Michigan, had recently applied for a
job in a great Chicago advertising agency. It "happened" that I got a letter one day from that agency,
offering me the job I wanted and directing me to
report in Chicago at once. It "happened" that I had
prayed for that job. But it "chanced" that I did not
have money enough to pay my local debts and buy
my ticket to the Windy City. I seemed stymied.

But—I did happen to have the habit of praying:
so I prayed about this. And what looked to me like a

miracle happened to me the very next day: the magazine to which I had sent my story awarded me a prize! It was only for nineteenth place, to be sure, but it was for $125, which at that time looked bigger to me than the full moon. It paid my debts and got me to Chicago and the new job.

But that was not the end of the matter. It happened that I had been trying for years to write and sell stories for young people to the good old Youth's Companion, then one of the best markets in that field. I had never sold to the Y.C. and I had a stack of "tries" at home that would fill a hatbox, with rejection slips to match. But it happened that the first prize in the story contest had been won by a Youth's Companion editor; so the Y.C. editors happened to be interested in the other prize winners too. And, lo and behold, they sent out a circular letter to all of us asking us to consider the Companion as a market for our future wares. I got one! I—*me*—I got a letter asking me to "consider" the Y.C. as a market!

You know how the ambitious beginner feels at first success in any field. I felt like that; only it seemed like a miracle to me, because I remembered that I had prayed.

Well, it was a series of coincidences, wasn't it? But I began to think that coincidence is like electricity: it follows the line of least resistance. I began to believe in my ability to write, and so began to write and sell my stories consistently; but I began

to believe too that a habit of praying sets up a line
of least resistance for blessings to flow over, blessings that seem like miracles.

I have never changed my mind about this. Other
"miracles" have happened to me. I have had so much
to be thankful for that I could write many more
stories of answered prayer and not use up my material. I haven't space here for more, because the
purpose of telling this story is not to recount wonders or brag about my blessings, but just to point out
a method of living that works.

I believe with all my heart that prayers are answered; not always exactly according to the words
of the prayer but always according to one's faith. I
know that prayers are answered in business, because I've been in business and received answers
more "striking" than lightning itself. I believe we
always get answers; we get what we ask for or
something better. I think you, whatever your business is, can and will get answers to your prayers if
you pray believing—believing enough to expect
them and to act on your expectation. Most of our
answers come in the form of ideas, inspirations,
directions to do something that will tend to answer
our own prayers.

Sometimes God does send miracles—miracles
of healing, of prosperity, of swift help in need—
in the form of circumstances that are wholly beyond our own control. Quite commonly He sends
"hunches" that enable us to use muscles and intelli-

gence; opportunities that look as if they could not
pay off in terms of our desires at all, but may pay
off in terms of somebody else's needs and desires.
But invariably your prayer and faith and effort,
all along a constructive line, will pay off for you,
in some form you will like. They will.

You have only to try it. You may think stories
of miracles are the "bunk"; that coincidences simply "happen"; that anybody who thinks God has
anything to do with them is simply a wishful thinker.
But you won't think so for long if you set up a
prayer line and go ahead living in expectation of
good, using all the powers you have been given to
promote good.

What is your problem? Have you tried prayer?
Have you tried persistent prayer—and persistent
faith, that won't quit when appearances seem to
indicate that you are a fool holding false hopes?
You are no fool if you trust God to keep faith with
you, to be as good as His word. God is better than
His word; for no words have ever been invented to
tell the half of it. After telling His disciples that He
would be leaving them Jesus said, "He that be-
lieveth on me, the works that I do shall he do also;
and greater *works* than these shall he do." He meant
it. Well, I am a humble disciple; I want to be His
disciple. Don't you? The resulting blessings are
"abundantly above all that we ask or think."

What would be the greatest and best blessing
that could come into your life? All right, pray for it.

Long ago Unity taught me a method of prayer that you must have heard about or read about: "Pray once for your heart's desire; and then, every time you think of it afterward, give thanks that you have the blessing you asked for. Pay no attention to appearances; however black they may look, never give up. Keep on giving thanks. God said, 'Before they call, I will answer.' Often you find that your answer is ready-made—God-made—was ready for you before you asked in words." This is a form of prayer that gets results. Try it. And don't quit. Make your life a prayer, as persistent as your breathing. Make it a prayer of thanksgiving, in words and in deeds.

Many people think that expectation of answer to prayer is dream stuff. But there is a perfect answer to this. You can prove that prayer is a power given you to use as truly as your lungs, your eyes, and your fingers were given you to use. Don't shrug this off; if you think you don't believe in it, try it anyway. Jesus said that if you have faith as a grain of mustard seed you can move mountains. Well, that should be about enough faith to induce anyone to pray. Go ahead and pray. Pray for what you really want, then do anything that occurs to you that will help bring about the answer to your prayer. And watch the results. Remember you prayed; watch for the answers. In a brief time you won't need anybody else to tell you that "God . . . is, and *that* he is a rewarder of them that seek after him."

Some men honestly think that any human being who has faith in prayer is "a nut." But what has that to do with it? If they are honest in their thinking, they are open to conviction; and you can help convince them if you will just have faith enough to pray, give thanks, "act as if it were impossible to fail," and keep on thanking God for answering before you ask. But better than that, you will convince yourself and have a more abundant life.

Does that sound selfish? Don't worry about that. If you find a more abundant life for yourself, your life will bless everybody that you meet—more than you can ask or think.

So They Want to Play Rough!

ANNE HOWARD WATERS

"THE ONLY Christian principle I've found really difficult to apply to my business," an eminently successful merchant remarked, "is the 'return-good-for-evil' teaching. It has taken self-discipline, a lot of prayer, and a few hard bumps to make me assimilate the idea thoroughly."

What this man was trying to say was that the reflex urge to "hit back," to retaliate in kind when we are hurt, is a human force with which to reckon. More accurately, it is a force to understand and recognize if we are to overcome it and thus clear the way for the honest, wholehearted application of Jesus' teachings, not only in business but in our daily, personal life as well.

It is so easy to justify retaliatory measures. "All right," we say, "I wanted to play the game fairly, to give the fellow (or the company) the same treatment I'd want to be given." And then, with what we delude ourselves into thinking is righteous indignation, we add, "But if he wants to get tough, I'll give him a dose of his own medicine!" And so the battle is on.

The answer to the return-good-for-evil problem lies in accepting oneself and the Christ Spirit within as a starting point—rather than behavior standards set up by others. Let the gentle, eternal goodness of the Christ Spirit shine through the quick anger, the outraged sense of injustice that puts in motion the machinery of retaliation. Use a positive affirmation such as *"I thank Thee, Father, for this opportunity to do Thy bidding,"* or *"The Christ Spirit within me guides me; its ever-present good permeates all my contacts and transactions."* One Truth student told me he found the old, simple blessing "God bless thee and keep thee," applied to the object of his momentary irritation, a reliable antidote and the basis for an immediate return of peace of mind.

This same merchant who found the return-good-for-evil principle difficult for a time finally came to its acceptance through reviewing an incident of his youth. As a boy he had lived in the slum district of one of our large cities, where poverty, disease, and general frustration were the basis for continuous violence, hatreds, and disputes. At the age of seven he had his first newspaper stand; by the time he was twelve, following the generally accepted pattern of a combination of physical force and "politics," he was undisputed "boss" of his territory.

A younger boy, a newcomer to the district, attempted to set up a competitive paper business. Following the only rule of survival he had ever known, the twelve-year-old put the younger boy out of business. A few months later the newcomer was sent to the reformatory—a member of a gang of juvenile delinquents picked up for stealing. Years later his picture appeared on the front page of every major newspaper in the country under the caption "Dangerous Killer."

The merchant regretted his part in what he felt was a circumstance leading to a man's destruction. In adult life he did all in his power to contribute to his fellow man's enlightenment and happiness. Looking back to those early years when he had not yet learned and accepted the Christian principles that were to make his life a happy and successful one, he was struck by the obviousness of cause and effect. Thus, in what he terms a cart-before-the-horse type of reasoning, he came to the acceptance of the wisdom and beauty of Jesus' admonition to return good for evil. He had only to contrast the dismal results of the eye-for-an-eye philosophy, as documented in the life he had known as a child, with the limitless good that resulted from the application of Truth principles to every phase of his life.

Another example I might cite is the experience of a friend, a hardware broker who successfully applied the principle of returning good for evil.

His territory covers five states; thus frequent and prolonged personal calls are impractical. To add problem to handicap he must keep not only his customers but also his suppliers (all of whom are situated a continent's breadth from him) satisfied with volume, profit, and representation.

A year ago one of his suppliers received a communication from a young salesman in the broker's most distant territory requesting permission to represent them. They replied that they were already adequately represented and anticipated no change, giving the young man the name and address of my friend, their Northwest broker. A few weeks later they received still another letter, attempting to "sell" them on a change in representation. The young man stated his qualifications in detail, listed other companies he represented and his advantageous connections, and hinted that he could give them much wider coverage than their present representative. Again they replied with a polite no.

The third letter was more insistent. The ambitious young man related alleged incidents of customer dissatisfaction with their present setup and commented that not only was their present representative disliked personally but that he had not been in the territory for over eight months (a statement that was without foundation in fact).

As each letter was received by the manufacturers it, together with a copy of their reply, was forwarded to my friend. The third was forwarded unanswered, with the sales managers notation: "This fellow seems bent on cutting your throat. We leave all correspondence with him to you from here on!"

The broker's reply to the young man was written only after a considerable period of prayer and deliberation. I believe you will agree that it is a thing of Christian beauty:

"I have for reply your letter of the 21st instant referred to me by my principals, the —— Manufacturing Company.

"In that letter you made certain allegations concerning my personality and ability. Please do not be embarrassed that they were forwarded to me. I'm quite sure you wrote in all sincerity and that, having entered this field rather recently and living within your territory, it may seem to you that my coverage is a bit 'spotty.' Frankly, the cost of traveling that area is prohibitive, and I must rely on two trips a year and correspondence for customer contacts. I realize, too, that one is not generally personally liked one hundred per cent. Therefore undoubtedly you were justified in that comment also.

"Lest you be too disappointed that you have failed to get this particular line, I point out that certain trade rules prevent the entire line being sold in your territory. At best you could only hope to represent the company on approximately thirty per cent of their products, all low-profit items.

"Although I'm what might be termed a 'grizzled veteran' after forty years in this business, I can still remember the uphill struggle of getting lines to represent—and then customers to buy them. If you will write me telling me frankly what you need to fill out your lines, I'll do everything I can to help you secure them. Almost daily I find it necessary to turn down an offer of representation—and if I could recommend you for your territory, I would be in a position to be of service, not only to you but to the company inquiring for representation.

"Next time I am in your city, won't you lunch with me so we can talk the matter over more fully? Perhaps I have a few customer contacts up your way that might be helpful. Meanwhile, however, feel free to write me.

"With kindest regards and best wishes for your success."

Do you feel, after reading this letter, that our broker took a "long chance"? Then perhaps the sequel to this letter will interest you. The young man did write him, with profuse and embarrassed apologies. The broker helped him secure three valuable lines (which did not conflict with the broker's own). On his next trip, he met the young man and spent several hours with him, even introducing him to a large buyer.

The result was, of course, that he made a friend instead of an enemy. He accepted the young man's original charges, unfair though they seemed, as constructive criticism and embarked on a mail campaign to keep in touch with his customers and prospects in that territory. This past six months his volume of business has been half again as great as it was for any previous similar period.

It is difficult at times to turn the other cheek— but with a little practice it can be done with gratifying results. Here are a few suggestions that may be helpful:

1. Accept the Christ Spirit within you as a starting point. Let it take over when the other fellow "plays rough."

2. Let the love and wisdom of the Christ Spirit quiet any human feeling of aggression and vengeance that often follows what you consider an unfair act.

3. "Love your enemies"—and you will have none!

4. Affirm your faith in the soundness and efficacy of Jesus' teachings at intervals during each day.

It's the Attitude

FRANCIS J. GABLE

O N A HOTEL ELEVATOR I heard several businessmen talking. They apparently were referring to one of their associates who had intimated that he had reached the limit of his usefulness to his firm.

One of the men said of him: "He thinks he is through," and at once another answered, "Well, if he thinks he is, he is so far as we are concerned. It's the attitude that counts."

It's the attitude. The man under discussion no doubt had the same intelligence he had shown for some time, the same ability that had probably been developed through years of experience in his work. But that intelligence and that ability were not enough. Neither was effective without the right mental attitude to vitalize it.

It matters not what the nature of our work may be, the matter of attitude is of prime importance. It may be called the mainspring or central power plant from which stems the impelling force that transmutes latent qualities into energy.

Suppose, for example, that you are a mechanic. You have a thorough knowledge of tools, machines, materials, and the principles that govern their use—

but you lack diligence or the desire to put your understanding to practical and consistent use. Your abilities are neutralized by lack of the proper attitude.

Perhaps you are in the selling end of business. You know your product, the manner of approach to a prospect. But with this knowing you exhibit an air of indifference or even of arrogance in your interviews. You could profitably exchange some of your external selling ability for an attitude of sincere interest in your customer's well-being. Lacking such an attitude, you are not worthy to be called a salesman. You need to cultivate the very spirit of salesmanship if you expect to rise above the plodding gait of a mere order taker.

You may occupy an executive position of greater or less importance, have all the details of your business at your finger tips, yet harbor the peculiar notion that you must maintain a dictatorial bearing toward those under your direction. (It is a sad commentary on business that men of this type are all too often placed in positions of authority.) You may be obsessed with the fear that they may take advantage of you in some fashion that would impair your dignity. Successful business has proved the fallacy of such an attitude because by pursuing it you defeat the very ends you hope to attain. Because relationships are so interwoven and complicated in the vastness of the field of modern business it becomes increasingly evident that it is the right attitude toward others that makes a man truly great.

Your position in the business world may be a very lowly one at the moment. The thing that you do may seem most unimportant in the broad scheme of industrial life. Your attitude is still of vital importance. Your advancement to greater work depends largely on your success in your present job. And your immediate success is measured by the attitude you exhibit.

If you are putting in just so many hours of time, if you are not trying to learn more of the details of your work, if you are careless or slipshod, if you foster the belief that progress is a matter of luck and that there isn't much chance for you, it is time that you snapped out of that attitude and found out what you are really there for. Your job can be an education, but you have to recognize the fact and avail yourself of it. It is your attitude that counts.

It is interesting to note that in some of our colleges increasing attention is being given to the development of this most important element in business, the attitude of the individual. Whereas in past years the entire instruction was devoted to the material aspects of commercial life, the present trend has to do with the businessman's outlook on life, on which his general attitude is founded. Often the establishment of a wholesome attitude to replace a negative one proves in itself to be the remedy for many difficulties that formerly had been regarded as wholly of physical origin.

If, as is here set forth, the attitude is so important, what specifically can be done about it? The devoutly religious businessman of course knows something of the efficacy of prayer in building the right attitude, but even prayer can be translated into action. Here are a few suggestions that anyone can put into practice as a means of improving his attitude:

Attitude toward self: Regardless of age, apparent lack of appreciation, or even the failure to measure progress, one needs to maintain a firm belief in himself. Such belief is not merely self-assumed; it is based on a recognition of the inherent divine power in man. The man referred to in the beginning of this article, who felt that he was through, had looked on himself only as a human machine with no reserve power on which to draw. As one of our great athletes has expressed it, you can accomplish a thing only as you have confidence in your ability to accomplish.

Attitude toward associates: Wherever two or more persons are employed in the same organization it is the expectation that each will complement, augment, or multiply the activities of every other one. It may appear at times that a worker is non-co-operative, or even obstructive. In spite of such appearance however no other worker can afford to maintain or express any attitude toward such a one other than of kindness and helpfulness. The worker who is out of line is alone responsible for his attitude and must experience the results of it. To deal

with him on a plane similar to his own merely makes
one liable to similar results.

Attitude toward workers: It may be well for one
who has been given any degree of authority to ana-
lyze the reason for this position. The only sound
reason why he has helpers of any type is that his
own work may be made easier and of greater effect.
If he could do personally everything that is needed
to be done, it is quite certain that helpers would not
be placed at his disposal.

It is obvious therefore that to make his own
work more effective and more important a person
in authority must adopt an attitude toward those
under him that will evoke the highest measure of
their support. A commanding attitude will not accomplish this, neither will an attitude of superiority.
The greatest leaders of men have proved that an attitude of oneness, of mutual interest and profit, will
alone fulfill the purpose of any authority that is
delegated.

Attitude toward employer or supervisor: The
progressive and satisfactory attitude of a worker
toward those in authority over him should in no
sense be one of inferiority or servility. It should naturally include the element of respect but it should be
an honest and merited respect, not one of compulsion
or fear. The most profitable attitude a worker can
hold toward his executive is one of gratitude based
on a recognition of the opportunity such relationship affords.

As a general rule, the man under whom you work holds that position of authority by reason of his ability. Of necessity, he must impart to you something of this ability if you are to be the proper assistant to him. In this respect he is your instructor and is being paid by your mutual employer for giving you instruction. In order to avail yourself of it to the highest degree you need to express an attitude of gratitude as suggested, and that expression is shown by your co-operation and your willingness to accept the instruction he has to offer. An attitude of patience, of receptivity, and above all of willingness to direct your own ability to the furtherance of your mutual good constitutes the success attitude.

Attitude toward the public: The essential features of this attitude are common to the salesman, the merchant, the manufacturer, and to any business owner or executive. The public is the ultimate authority on kind and quantity of merchandise or service; the public is the paymaster and the source of profit and dividend. And because it holds these enviable and vital positions, the attitude toward the public is of vast importance.

It can never be one of indifference or of fear or of flattery if right relations are to be established and maintained. It is essentially an attitude of understanding interest, of a sincere desire to know what the public wants and how its need may best be fulfilled.

Notwithstanding the oft-repeated slogan "The

customer is always right," the attitude toward the public need involve no compromise of principle, no injury to pride. The demand of the consumer and the supply of that demand are but the two ends of the channel that carries the flow of business; each is a component part of the same thing.

The attitude toward the public then should be that of oneness, of understanding, as has been said, and this attitude can be enduringly based only on friendliness and love. Find a place of business, great or small, that consistently reveals such an attitude and you find a successful, a profitable, and a joyous business.

We have tried to suggest that in whatsoever direction you look in business the fact is brought home with increasing force that the man in the elevator voiced an eternal truth when he said, "It's the attitude that counts."

Words That Can Change Your Life

HAROLD S. KAHM

F ROM TIME immemorial men have sought magic
words, by uttering which they could summon
riches, fame, power, love, or any other great
thing that they might desire. Thousands of ancient
legends, fairy stories, and fictional histories have told
of wise men, witches, and fairy queens who have
had command of secret phrases that could accomplish miracles. The ancient Hebrews, or at least some
of them, believed that God had a secret name, which,
when uttered, would invoke His presence materially.

So it is that thousands of years before the development of modern psychological knowledge, human
beings of virtually every race and place recognized,
however dimly, the potential power of the spoken
word to change their circumstances and their lives.

We know now that they were on the right track,
at least. There is no power in *abracadabra* or in
any other nonsensical word or phrase, but there is tremendous magic in ordinary words that we can employ in our daily living.

Jesus was keenly aware of the mysterious power
of the spoken word when He warned men that they
could be defiled by the words they spoke, and that
they would be judged by every word they uttered.

Modern psychology has proof of the absolute logic of His advice: other people judge us by our words; but what is far more significant, we judge ourselves. Let a healthy man state, "I am sick" repeatedly, and he will eventually judge himself to be sick, and he will be sick. Men have talked themselves into the grave. Conversely, optimistic men, stricken by the shadow of illness, have talked themselves into radiant health. Financially poor men have talked themselves into material prosperity by way of new and better-paid jobs or greatly increased business.

The human mind, within whose unfathomable recesses dwells each man's share of God's presence, is the mightiest force man can use. The mind's influence on the body, on other minds, on circumstances, on itself, is nothing short of fantastic. Conscious thought is only one of its attributes. Just as the visible portion of a floating iceberg represents only one-ninth of the iceberg's total dimensions, so does our use of human consciousness and thought represent but a fraction of the potential of the human mind. What enormous powers lie secret within that vast unknown? Modern science has afforded some valuable and positive clues.

It is within this subconscious area that faith dwells. A man may say to himself, "I believe!" and yet, if his belief is shallow, superimposed, existing only in his conscious mind, it proves to be inoperative; it doesn't work. It has failed to reach beneath the conscious surface of his intelligence; it is not rooted in the depths of his subconscious mind, where he truly lives and has his power.

Jesus, as had others before Him, referred to this subconscious human kingdom as the "heart." An Old Testament wise man said, "As he [man] thinketh in his heart, so *is* he." Jesus stated, "Where your treasure is, there will your heart be also."

A man cannot deliberately think "in his heart," yet what he thinks in his heart determines his life, his circumstances, his health, everything that concerns him and his fellow men. A man can have faith effectively only if this faith dwells in his heart, but how can he implant it there?

Too often men mistake an emotion for inner conviction. Stirred by a sermon, written or spoken, that drives home to him the power of faith and of love, the man tells himself: "It is true! It is wonderful! I believe!" At the time his heart seems to be stirred, but it is not necessarily stirred into creative, forceful action. It may not even be really convinced; it may, in fact, remain virtually untouched.

It is as though a man attempted to turn on an electric light by will power alone, without touching his hand to the switch.

This is what has been finally discovered: the subconscious mind, the "heart," can be and is reached by the words we speak. Every word we utter, or entertain in silent thought, is a directive that cannot be ignored. Thus, a man who says in his conscious mind, "I have faith," automatically sets up within his heart a mechanism that also can say, "I have faith."

If this man would make this statement and no other, there would be this one great directive and one inevitable result. The man would have faith, and his faith could move mountains.

But today he says, "I have faith" and an hour or a day later he countermands his statement by saying, "I am afraid," or "What's the use?" or "I don't feel well."

Consistency is the keynote to success. "If therefore thine eye be single," said the Master, "thy whole body shall be full of light." Let your statements, the words that you utter aloud or in thought, be of a pattern: positive. Each of these positive words is like a light switch. You will understand this implication best if you have ever played a pinball game. Pinball has a panel with many numbers; you win the game when your catapulted metal balls have made the necessary contacts and all of the numbers have been lighted. Then your pinball victory is complete. In the great game of self-mastery and the quest for absolute faith the victory is yours when your statements, constantly repeated, have, as it were lighted up all the lights in your heart so that your whole body is full of light.

Every positive statement you make turns on one of these lights.

Every negative statement you make turns one of them off.

The Truth student knows these positive statements as affirmations and denials. He affirms the good and denies the evil. And in this method there is almost fantastic achievement. Let a man be ever so ill or hopeless or discouraged or frustrated or unsuccessful or unhappy and let him place a curb upon his words, so that every statement he utters or thinks is positive—and then slowly, steadily, inevitably, the black shadow grows smaller, smaller, and then vanishes utterly. There can be no blackness where the sun shines unimpeded.

Has he merely hypnotized himself into believing what is not so? Is he ill, but believes himself well? Are his circumstances unaltered, but he merely tells himself they are altered? If this were so, it would be a mockery. But it is not so. The human mind wherein dwells the unlimited power of God has the power to effect all changes, material and spiritual. It commands the body and the body obeys; it commands circumstances and the circumstances are altered. It is not the mind that does this; it is not the man who does this. It is the power of God, that dwells within the mind and the heart, that does it. Said Jesus, "I can of myself do nothing"; "the Father abiding in me doeth his works."

This subject is as vast and as mysterious as the universe. But we can understand one thing that we must understand, and that is this: Your power to have the quality of faith that moves mountains; your power to believe in God and to secure prompt answers to your prayers, the granting of all good desires—these are all concerned with your use of words, words thought and words uttered aloud. If these words are positive, and only positive, the positive response in your heart will light up as a man's voice echoes between mountains, automatically.

The words that can change your life are the words you speak in the morning over the breakfast table, the words you utter all through the day and evening. They are all the words you speak, and the words you think that are called thoughts.

The rules for changing your life are simple: Speak only words that express positive thoughts. Say no word that expresses a negative thought of any kind.

What is a negative thought? It is any thought that acknowledges or suggests lack of any kind, or anger, fear, envy, jealousy, or any other thing that is not compatible with goodness, or "God-ness."

What is a positive thought? It is any thought that acknowledges fulfillment, prosperity, success, health, love, or any other idea that is wholly compatible with goodness.

Each word you speak will have its effect, according to its positive or negative nature. This is inescapable. Positive words will bring about positive circumstances for you in the material world.

You will not find it easy at first. How habitually do we deny God by denying the good! Deny evil and the shadow of evil! Affirm the good! By this method is the word "made flesh," and "Thou shalt also decree a thing, and it shall be established unto thee."

Your words can change your life.

Your words will change your life!

From this moment forward, and for all time, allow yourself to utter not a single word, unless that word is positive in character.

Let your words always, always declare and decree the good condition that you desire, as though it were already an accomplished fact; let your words deny the absence of any lack, and let them deny the shadow of evil, even though that evil seems to be a present reality. "Judge not according to the appearance."

When out of lifelong habit you find yourself inadvertently making negative statements, recall them and deny them; use powerful positive statements to replace them!

Once you have established the new habit of speaking only positive words and thinking only positive thoughts, your faith in God will have become absolute and His response to your prayers will be swift and perfect.

The words that can and will change your life are the ordinary, daily words of your life—the words that will bring you consciously into God's presence, into His abundant, limitless blessings.

Such is the power of words, the magic of words.

No Age Limit

SUSAN SCOTT

AGAIN AND AGAIN it has been said that this is an age designed for youth. Men and women with years of experience in the business world complain that they are being replaced by younger workers. Many who have been discharged and thus forced to go the rounds of employment offices have been told: "We do not take on anyone over thirty-five. Sorry, but that is the rule here." In some places the age limit for employment is thirty.

Those of us who are over thirty-five ask ourselves why employment should be confined to younger people. Shall we accept the theory that we are getting beyond the age of usefulness and that the future is hopeless for us?

After all, God did not make the rules under which employment managers work. They were made by man, and all things made by man are subject to change and to adjustment. God's laws are greater than man's limitations. Defeat is an unknown quantity to the man or woman who trusts in the omnipotent power and unlimited reserves of the spiritual universe rather than in the limitations of the material world.

Some years ago I found myself out of employment. No matter where I went younger women were preferred for the openings available. Advertisements I should have liked to answer drew the age limit just below my own age. For the first time in my career the future was shaken with uncertainty. I became afraid of failure; then I became bitter and resentful.

I had helped to build up my old position. I looked on it as mine. I had not dreamed that it would pass into other hands. True, no higher salary or advancement was possible in it, but I felt that it was my job; I had no desire to yield it to another. But a time came when I was put into a position that virtually forced my resignation.

I listened to the commiseration of my friends. To an extent it was comforting to know that they realized I had been forced out of a position where I had proved my ability, but gradually I came to recognize a new note in their sympathy. They were impressing on me the fact that I should realize that I was not as young as I used to be.

When anyone's optimism gets a blow of this kind, one of two things is likely to happen: either he goes down to defeat or he rises from the trial stronger and more determined than ever. I realize now that had it not been for my study of Truth I might have been a broken woman then—in my early forties. But for years it has been my practice when things went wrong to sit down and try to figure out wherein I had come short of fulfilling spiritual laws. I tried to see whether God might not have a plan for my life that was greater and broader than my limited vision.

One day I was poring over a favorite periodical when my attention was focused on the sentence "I seek employment only in proving my ability, for success is reckoned only in terms of growth." That sentence stayed with me and gave me a lot to ponder over. I asked myself, "How can I prove my ability when the opportunity to prove it is lacking?"

To be honest with myself, I had to admit presently that even though I had not found an opportunity I could not say that no opportunity existed. The fact that I do not own any genuine pearls does not prove that there are no genuine pearls in the world. On the contrary there are thousands of them. So too there must be countless opportunities if I could but find them.

I decided to look more closely at that sentence. One of the first steps for me to take in seeking employment was to prove my ability. I asked myself what my most useful ability was.

During my time at home I had been doing freelance writing, which had kept the wolf from the door and occupied my time, but I longed to be back in the business world with the security of a job. Now I was challenged to appraise my ability and decide in what direction it might lead me.

Most writers are dreamers and inclined to be impractical, but I was always interested in the business end of my work. Once an outstanding man in an advertising agency had told me when I said to him that selling was something I was sure I could not do: "That's what you think! I have met few people who can do indirect selling as well as you do. Your enthusiasm is being wasted on the writing side of the picture."

I began to wonder how I could use my enthusiasm. Actually it had never before occurred to me that I should try to use it. The idea immediately brought out of my consciousness another one: Advertising is a combination of writing and selling. Why not try my luck there? But advertising is a very complicated business, and I had always understood that breaking into it was very difficult.

Here is something that Truth does for anyone who studies it faithfully. When an idea fastens itself in his mind he knows that it is not impossible, that nothing undertaken in the spirit of faith is impossible. So I began to study various kinds of advertising writing. I experimented with radio scripts and with magazine advertisements. There were times when I began to think I hadn't much ability to prove to myself, yet each new effort opened new avenues of thought.

There was one product to which I gave a great deal of time and thought. A friend of mine was interested in it and gave a lot of time to discussing with me an idea that had occurred to me for a new kind of demonstration work. He advised me to present it to the company that was behind the product. Perhaps they would let me try out my idea.

Now I was tempted to pray that the way would open for me to secure that work. But I had long ago grasped the fact that one must not pray for a thing but for a principle; not for any particular job but for the best place of service to which God might direct one. So I prayed long and earnestly that I might get work where I could prove my ability and give happy service in the best way.

Then the miracle happened. Anyhow it was like a miracle to me. My neighbor came over one day and told me about an opening in his firm available to whoever could suggest a good idea for promoting a certain product. I immediately suggested adapting my idea to this product. After some discussion we worked out a logical plan, and arranged an interview for me with the president of the firm.

The result of this interview was that I obtained a position far better and more interesting than I ever dreamed I could hold. It meant I could be at home with my family instead of traveling most of the time, and it was work requiring such a wide knowledge of human values that it could be handled only by a person of my age and experience!

The spirit of faith was with me, and my success was sure. Never again will I feel that there is no place for me in the business world.

Some reader may say: "Oh, but you had natural

ability to start with. Your writing experience made it possible for you to land a good job like that." True, but if I had not made a special effort to exploit my business ability as applied to writing, the way could not have opened for me. I know many writers with minds more brilliant than mine who have become financially embarrassed and dependent on others long before their retirement age.

God's ways are greater than our ways, and His resources are beyond our comprehension. When we have been given opportunity for happy service we must grow with our work and not settle into a rut. A place in the business world is ours only as long as we continue to prove our ability and then wait on the Lord to extend our opportunity, for our success is truly reckoned in terms of growth, not dollars and cents. When we are doing this, we are too busy to notice the passing of the years and we are too wise to look on any job as our own exclusive creation. God has other and larger fields of service waiting for us when we are ready to go to them.

The Greatest among You

CLINTON E. BERNARD

O NCE UPON A TIME there was a reformer who set about preparing a lecture that he hoped would be his masterpiece. He worked in his study, which was equipped with most of the comforts that business had been able to devise. He made notes, using his fountain pen, which business had made and sold to him with a guarantee that it would last him a lifetime. Presently he called his secretary over the interoffice communication system that business had installed. She took his dictation and then transcribed her notes on a typewriter that business had made.

That evening the man set out to fill his lecture engagement. He did not have to walk; he was transported comfortably to the place in a fine automobile that business had developed. His lecture hall was on the sixty-third floor of a skyscraper that business had built, but he did not have to walk up to it; he was whisked there by an elevator that business had made and installed. Although the evening was a sweltering one, the hall was kept perfectly comfortable by an air-conditioning unit that business had provided. The lecturer delivered a stirring address on the evil nature of business, and the audience, all of whom derived their living directly or indirectly from business, cheered and cheered. Then he went down in the elevator and got into his automobile. He stopped at a restaurant and ate a good dinner of food that business had processed. Then he went home to sleep soundly in his comfortable bed that business had constructed. He had given business a real lambasting and he was very happy about it.

It doesn't make sense.

Why do we lambaste business, especially big business, and indict all of it as evil?

To prosper and grow large a business must have many loyal customers. Why does a customer become loyal to a company? Because he is convinced that it gives him a larger value for his money than he could get from its competitors. A business outgrows its competitors by outserving them. This is certainly true where the competitive system prevails. But what about monopolies?

The Aluminum Company of America has often been cited as enjoying a monopoly in its line in the United States. For many years the company was the only one producing virgin aluminum in this country. It was called "an octopus of business" and most of the other invidious names that have been applied to big companies. The price of aluminum might have been expected to soar under such circumstances. What are the facts in the case?

Long before aluminum was made available in

commercial quantities anybody could see that it was
a metal with a bright future. In malleability and
ductility it was almost the equal of gold; it was almost nontarnishable; in tensile strength it ranked
with cast iron; it combined well with alloys. Most
important of all, it was extremely light. The metal
was not found in its pure state however, and extrac-
tion of it was extremely difficult and costly. Napo-
leon III ate with aluminum forks and spoons, thus
outdoing the aristocrats who could obtain only gold
forks and spoons. The metal was quoted then at
about $545 a pound, though the supply was usually
reckoned in ounces or in even smaller units. In 1855
ingots of aluminum were exhibited as a curiosity at
the Paris Exposition.

Shortly before 1890 there was organized a firm
that eventually became the Aluminum Company of
America (popularly known as "Alcoa"). An improved process for extracting the metal had been
developed. By 1899 the price of aluminum was down
to $2 a pound. In 1904 the price was thirty-three
cents a pound; in 1911, twenty-two. In the latter
year moreover Alcoa was the only producer of aluminum in the United States. In December, 1941, the
price of aluminum ingots was twenty cents a pound.
The New International Encyclopedia remarks of
aluminum that "the price has decreased almost in
proportion to the increased production."

The writer is not trying to boost Alcoa stock. He
has none of it. He mentions the company here only

to illustrate that even a monopoly finds it most profitable to serve well and at a moderate profit.

Alcoa risked money in a pioneer field. It was entitled to a good profit. The men at the head of the concern knew economics however and realized that any attempt to extract and maintain an exorbitant profit would be a poor business policy. Aluminum, with its lightness and its other distinctive good qualities, was creating a bigger demand for light and useful metals. If they put the price of aluminum too high they would invite new competitors to enter the field; also they would stimulate research into cheaper and lighter metals to take the place of aluminum. They avoided this mistake—but they could not avoid consequences brought about by war.

War has an insatiable appetite for metals. In World War II there was a frenzied demand for metals suitable for use in the manufacture of airplanes and other materials. Not enough aluminum could be produced with available facilities. But supply inevitably tends to keep up with demand. Magnesium, which is even lighter than aluminum, was produced in enormously increased quantities. Beryllium, which is much lighter than magnesium, also popped up as a competitor.

No monopoly that restricts trade has ever prevailed for long; no such monopoly ever can prevail for long. It would be against divine laws and economic laws. In all business, from the corner grocery to the largest of corporations, they take good care of the trade or they lose it. There is no appeal from this law. It is inexorable—and divinely useful.

But did the competition offered by new metals cause Alcoa to plan to reduce its production after the war? Such is not the spirit of modern business. The company put into effect a program calling for expenditure of a million dollars a year in its research laboratories looking for new ways in which aluminum can serve mankind better. It made discoveries that are working a revolution in airplane design and performance. And it had a shoal of new ideas worked out and in storage, awaiting the return to normal life and opportunity that followed the war.

Such is the pattern of successful business. Not only must a successful company serve well but it must look for new ways to serve better. Such looking ahead may begin with only the motive of profit, but anybody who is keen enough to succeed in modern business is keen enough to perceive the deeper relationship, the spiritual and inevitable relationship, between good service and good business. Good business is good service; the better the service the more successful the business.

How many persons can justly lay claim to such altruistic motives in their private life? The fact is that spirituality is increasing in business faster than in private life. Business is actually, if unintentionally, a missionary to teach the discerning that the principles laid down by Jesus are the foundation of success in any line.

The tendency to flagellate business springs at least partly from an old and ridiculous piece of snobbery. Through ancient and medieval times the quality folk lived on the fruits of the labors of their slaves and serfs. They held business to be a very low way of making a living; organized banditry and warfare were more to their taste. So some drones, living in the past, still scorn the workers.

Part of the stigma placed on business is political. Politicians have found big business a convenient whipping boy. Apparently they reason that anything which has attained unusual stature is evil. By that line of reasoning a United States senator should be an archfiend. Big business, impersonal because of its very size, has seldom bothered to deny the charges made against it.

There has been bad practice—sometimes criminal practice—in some large firms, certainly. There have been scandals in the church also. Shall we on that account ban religious worship? If we proscribed every human activity that has ever been associated with evil we would be reduced to twiddling our thumbs—or perhaps even that would be under the ban.

It is time for us to think the truth about business. It is not something apart from us, something belonging to a small group vaguely designated as "they." It is a part of our pattern of civilization and basically good. There was a need of humble and willing servants, efficient specialists, to help the people live happily and comfortably; business is the result. But good servants are likely to become more important than their masters, so it was impossible to maintain invidious old social distinctions. The serving class and the ruling class intermarried and became all one family as it were. All do some ruling and some serving. And this is the proper way, the divine way.

Business is our business. Business is our good friend; it merits the loyalty and the respect due any good friend. If it fails sometimes to keep to its proper, high standards, we can and should help it with good precept and good example just as we would help any other friend or servant.

We are divinely enjoined to be thankful for the blessings we enjoy. We depend on business for our physical living, for the comforts and luxuries that make life more pleasant. Why should it not have our praise, our blessing, the same as any other good servant? Why should we not stress its good qualities and seek to improve the qualities that need improving?

Art galleries and concerts and travel and other cultural pursuits are important, but they are not the best of life. The best of life is to be found in our everyday expression of life, our regular business. If we call this expression evil we rob ourselves of joy and legitimate growth; if we call it good and suit our action to the word we enhance our joy and our usefulness.

Business is fundamentally good. Why not give it the respect due goodness?

Today all of us live on the labors of the servant called business. Anybody who punishes this servant unfairly is punishing himself and is certain to feel the pain eventually.

Business, being extremely practical, is learning that the laws laid down by Jesus form the best code for successful trade. It would probably be true to say that Christianity has made greater strides in business in the past fifty years than in any other field, including the church.

Successful firms are scrupulously honest; this is the rule rather than the exception. It is becoming common for people to be far more Christian in their business than in their private life. Business success demands humility and integrity. Most people give more courtesy to customers than to their relatives and close friends; they turn the other cheek to customers, although they may be suing a mate for divorce on grounds of incompatibility. Trade, once reviled as low caste, is now an outstanding exponent and teacher of Christianity. Business appreciates a good thing—and Christianity is the best.

"But he that is greatest among you shall be your servant."

Building Personal Good Will

WILFERD A. PETERSON

GREAT INDUSTRIES consider good will their most valuable possession. It is the fire under their boilers. It is the light in their windows. It is the energy that makes their factories hum with activity. Without good will plants are useless, machines are motionless, men are idle. Good will is the lifeblood of commerce. Industries value good will in millions of dollars.

The other day I heard the president of a large organization making a remark about one of his junior executives. "That boy is going places," he said. "He is one in a thousand!" The young man is succeeding because he is building up personal good will. Each of us, as an individual, manufactures some kind of service that he tries to sell to others. How far we go in our profession or in our industry depends in large measure on the amount of good will we create for ourselves. Good will is as valuable to you as the good will of General Motors is to that great organization. You should guard your good will as zealously as a giant corporation guards its good will. Your success and happiness in life are largely dependent on the amount of good will you have on deposit in your bank of living.

Your good will is the total of all the good thoughts and favorable attitudes people have toward you. Every word or act of yours builds or destroys good will. If you were to put a dollar value on your personal good will, how much would it be worth to you today?

Most of our great business firms started small. They grew great by multiplying their friendships, expanding their good will. You can live a bigger life by multiplying your friendships, expanding your personal good will.

A vice-president of General Motors, put into two sentences the formula by which business firms may increase their good will. "First, find out what people like about you and do more of it. Second, find out what people do not like about you and do less of it." You and I can use this same formula in building our personal good will.

For my own guidance I have written out five principles for increasing my fund of personal good will.

1. *Be a man of character.* People pay little favorable attention to the man who does not have a reputation for honesty. His words fall on deaf ears. Like the boy who cried wolf, even when he does speak the truth it is discounted. The words of the honest man, on the other hand, are charged with power. He has a reputation for honesty, and people give him their undivided attention. Honesty, sincerity, square dealing, justice, tolerance, faith, courage, these are

foundation qualities that attract people. They generate confidence and faith. No amount of noise or shouting can compensate for lack of character. As Emerson put it, "what you *are* stands over you the while, and thunders so that I cannot hear what you say to the contrary." To win and hold good will a man must be genuine. As a boy I memorized a little rhyme that I have always remembered. It goes like this:

"Don't be veneer stuck on with glue,
  Be solid mahogany all the way through!"

2. *Rise above retaliation.* A person does not make friends by going around with a chip on his shoulder. He makes enemies, and one who desires to increase his fund of personal good will cannot afford enemies. Enemies talk and act against us. They tear us down in the minds of those whom we wish to think well of us. Every enemy we make is a salesman trying to "unsell" us to those we wish to influence. If we wish to build good will we must stop creating ill will. We must learn to keep sweet on the inside. We must resolve to rise above hatred, resentment, jealousy, revenge. We must remember that whenever we "knock" another person we have landed a blow at our own good will. We must strive to be known as a man too big to be petty. We must measure our relations with our fellows by the Golden Rule.

3. *Maintain friendships.* Personal good will depends not only on making new friends, but also on

holding old friends. It means taking time to write letters to friends at a distance. One executive I know has made it a habit to write a letter to an old friend the first thing each morning. It is a constructive habit that has enriched his life. The telephone is right at your elbow and a telephone call to a friend from whom you haven't heard in a long time will renew the bonds of fellowship. Hold on to your friends, and they will spread out across the face of the earth to sing your praises. Someone has said that if you see a friend slipping away from you, you should drop everything and bring him back, for friendship is the most valuable thing in life. The way to keep yourself alive in the minds of your friends everywhere is by reminding them that you are alive, by contacting them regularly through the mails, over the telephone, or in person.

4. *Radiate dynamic good will.* Dynamic good will and God's will seem to me to be synonymous terms. When you open your life to God's will you become a channel for expressing the highest good. As you send out thoughts of dynamic good will to others you create a magnetic personal atmosphere that will attract others to you. People will seek you out because in your presence they will be given a mental lift and will be inspired to make their lives worth while. As you meet all people in a spirit of good will, you will find their attitudes toward you changing from possible antagonism and friction to friendliness and co-operation. Dynamic good will

is mental sunshine thawing out the ice of misunderstanding, suspicion, and fear. Like attracts like. It is a spiritual law that as you project dynamic good will toward others you will set in motion mighty currents that will bring in floods of personal good will to you.

5. *Make a name for yourself.* Your deeds speak for you; therefore set a record for excelling, for doing your tasks superbly, for being a great producer. Strive to make your name stand for leadership in your profession or industry. Strive to do good in addition to doing well. Spend your energies to make a better world. The deeds you do will write a vivid advertisement of your ability, manhood, and ideals in the minds of those in your sphere of life.

It all comes down at last to this: If you want the good will of others you must earn it. Whether your personal good will is worth thirty cents or a million dollars depends on you. It is a reflection of what you are!

The Daily Power Builder

RETTA M. CHILCOTT

W HEN A PERSON starts to do physical work he usually spends some time in getting ready before entering upon the actual labor. For example, a carpenter clears his bench of rubbish and unnecessary material before he begins a new task. When a seamstress begins to work on a new dress she clears away from her machine scraps of cloth and thread left over from the dress she has just finished. These processes of preparation are essential to the doing of efficient work.

Clearing the mental field of action is equally important when we attempt to perform tasks of a mental nature. Before starting the day's work in an office the worker should clear his mind of all thoughts that detract from his efficiency in the work he is to do. It is equally important that he gives his mind positive, upbuilding food, or thought, before he takes up the duties of the day.

Such a process is constructive preparation; it tunes the mind to higher efficiency. If meditation on a proper statement is persisted in for five minutes each morning, a worker will find that he can work faster and better than ever before.

The habit of morning meditation in an office is

not a matter of creed or of doctrine; the practice can be put into effect in any business and will result in great benefit and profit to both employer and employee. The writer has observed workers of the most unpromising types in an office where morning meditation was made a regular practice. In a few weeks some of them improved so much in manner, appearance, and conduct that they seemed to be different persons.

The fact that a firm has enough interest in and consideration for its employees to co-operate with them in this way at the beginning of the day's work promotes a spirit of loyalty in the entire force. The workers soon realize the benefits they receive. They are able to do their work with greater ease and with less fatigue in mind and body. No one wants to be tired, yet carrying unnecessary burdens in the mind induces more weariness than any other cause.

A period of morning meditation is a wonderfully harmonizing influence in an office. A disturbed, distressed mind will cause a worker to stir up discord, when otherwise conditions would be perfectly harmonious. Any manager knows that discord in an organization causes unnecessary expense and loss. It is a well-known fact that both workers and executives can think more rapidly and clearly if they focus all their attention on one thing at a time. One way to learn to concentrate is to start the day right.

The first five minutes of the working day in an office should be set aside as a period of silence or meditation, in which everyone in the organization, from the highest to the lowest, should be expected to take part. The workers should be encouraged to relax their bodies, to sit in a comfortable position, and to clear their minds of all the problems and outside affairs that have occupied their thoughts. Then a wholesome, constructive thought for meditation should be suggested, one that will appeal to all. A statement that experience has shown to be very helpful is: *"I begin each day's work with joy and thanksgiving, knowing that I shall find unlimited opportunity for growth and success."* Those of a more devout turn of mind will probably want to use a statement such as this: *"There is only one presence and one power in my life: God, the good, omnipotent."*

Use of an affirmation that puts joy into the mind gives energy to mind and body. Realization of gratitude causes one to want to give freely of his ability. Added joy, strength, and satisfaction in service come to him who realizes that he improves himself and increases his ability while he serves.

Employers who have given no previous thought to a meditation period in the morning may be inclined to object to such an innovation on the grounds that it would entail considerable loss of time, especially in a large organization. In making their objections these employers forget that what they are buying from their employees is not time but efficiency and accomplishment. Every good businessman recognizes that a well-poised mind is valuable because poise is one of the requisites of efficiency.

Employers everywhere are seeking efficient workers, workers who can concentrate. Men and women are striving to learn how to work better. A young person will spend years in school and in college, at a cost of thousands of dollars, all for the purpose of attaining greater efficiency. Yet instruction and aids on concentration (one of the essentials of efficiency) are given little attention in either the educational or the business world.

It is impossible for the body to be in two places at the same time. It is equally impossible for the mind to focus on two things at the same time. The attention may move with lightning-like rapidity and almost imperceptibly from one subject to another, but there is an instant, while the change of mental focus is taking place, in which the mind is centered on neither subject. Such moving from one thing to another lessens mental efficiency, just as the work performed by a carpenter would be curtailed if he ran constantly from one job to another.

The manager of any group of workers can demonstrate for himself that a proper beginning of the day's work will go a long way toward making more efficient the individuals under his supervision. We who have used the plan for years and know the influence it has on the workers can forejudge the degree of efficiency that will characterize each day's labor by observing the attention given to the morning meditation.

Dissolving the Deadlocks

WORRAL G. SONASTINE

NOT LONG ago I was talking with John R. Tipton, member of the International Executive Board of Transport Workers Union of America, C. I. O. He firmly believes in the practice of prayer at the conference table. "On several occasions," he said, "I have seen antagonistic attitudes melt away as the chaplain offered a prayer for success and harmony at the conference table. There is something irresistible about the power of prayer at such times."

On several occasions during the past few months I have been asked this question: "Do you think Jesus could solve the labor-management problems if He were here today?" The question is usually followed by others of a similar nature: "Just how would He go about it? What would He do?"

The answer to these questions is being enacted every day in various parts of the country. Jesus, in Spirit, is solving the labor-management problems of today. His teachings and recommendations are fast becoming the guiding principles in all labor-management discussions. Those who participate in these discussions are realizing more and more the importance of seeing the other fellow's point of view. The Golden Rule is more widely accepted to-day than ever before.

From my own observation, I find that at least eighty per cent of the proposals made by labor leaders are offered in the sincere belief that they are just. The same is true regarding the proposals made by management. When both sides in a controversy sincerely believe they are right, counterproposals are usually made and the differences worked out through the process of bargaining. If and when an absolute deadlock is reached, though, something has to give, or perhaps somebody has to give, before the disagreement can be settled. Here is where the love and wisdom of Jesus, if sought through prayer, can be miraculously helpful. The Master said, "Where two or three are gathered together in my name, there am I in the midst of them."

In Reader's Digest, Norman Vincent Peale told of an incident that occurred in Detroit which might well be used as a pattern for working out other problems of a similar nature. The leaders of a large union called a mass meeting in Cadillac Square one afternoon at 4 o'clock. The police commissioner refused to grant a permit for the meeting because in his opinion downtown traffic was too dangerously heavy at that hour. The union officials insisted that the meeting would proceed on schedule. It looked as though there would be trouble, perhaps bloodshed, if the police tried to prevent the meeting from being held. The mayor was out of the city, but the acting mayor called several clergymen to attend the final conference between the police and union leaders. No agreement could be reached, but just as the conference was about to break up one of the ministers suggested that they all pray over the matter. Everyone accepted the suggestion, and some time was spent in prayer.

"Fifteen minutes later," says Doctor Peale, "they sat again at the conference table. The acting mayor cleared his throat. 'How will it do if the meeting is held in Cadillac Square, but at 6 o'clock instead of 4?'

" 'Suppose we hold our meeting only at one end of the square so as not to tie up traffic?' the union leader countered.

"The huge mass meeting at 6 p.m. that Tuesday was a completely peaceful affair."

Prayer breaks down resistance and removes friction. It brings understanding and enables men to see beneath the surface of things. Without understanding we often act in conflict with God's laws and thereby defeat our own purposes. This matter of defeating our own purposes by acting contrary to God's laws reminds me of an incident that occurred in the community where I lived when I was a boy.

Ezra Higgins, a parsimonious old farmer of my acquaintance, had two young lads working for him as hired hands. One evening he told the boys he would give them a quarter apiece if they would not eat any supper that night. They agreed and went to bed hungry in order to earn the extra change. Next morning when they came to breakfast old Higgins was waiting for them.

"Jest decided," he said, "that you boys can't have any breakfast 'less you give back the money I gave you last night."

Chic Sale, the beloved character actor, told me a story about Grandma Tucker, who had been a neighbor of Chic's when he was a young man. It seems that Grandma's sixteen-year-old niece was leaving home to be hired girl for a family on the other side of the county. When she had her things packed and was ready to leave Grandma called her aside to offer some parting advice.

"Now, Bessie," said the grandmother, "you git all you kin and do as little as you kin."

When Chic finished telling the story, he laughed and said: "You know, Grandma Tucker tried awfully hard to get ahead financially but she never quite succeeded. She just couldn't seem to get it through her head that you only get out of life a heaping measure of what you put into it—so it's no wonder she spent her last days in the county infirmary."

Like Grandma Tucker, my old friend Higgins spent his last days in the county infirmary. He would certainly have been a poor employer to represent management in a dispute with labor. His ideas were contrary to the cosmic laws of justice, and consequently they were doomed to failure right from the start. Grandma Tucker's ideas were just as wrong. As a representative of labor, she would have brought disaster down upon the very people she wanted to help. It was logical that these two misguided persons should end up in poverty. Anyone who acts against the laws of God in any realm of life may expect failure in that particular field, and can never achieve true happiness or success in any field.

In my discussions with John R. Tipton he told me that labor was becoming more and more aware of the fact that the welfare of its members depends on the welfare of the company. "It is also a fact," he said, "and we are aware of it, that the welfare of both labor and management is dependent on the welfare of the general public. With these thoughts in mind, we earnestly try to keep our motives right and our demands just. After all, we don't want to kill the goose that lays our golden egg."

All too often the average person feels that he or she can do nothing to improve labor-management relations. We feel somehow that the efforts of one person can have little effect on such momentous problems. This is a mistake. Every worth-while thing that is ever accomplished is first conceived in the mind of an individual. It is then usually followed through and carried out by other individuals. This is the procedure through which every great and good movement comes into being. It is the way in which you and I can help to improve labor-management relations in the world about us. We can, if we are ever involved in a labor dispute of any kind, pray for guidance. We can try to see the other fellow's point of view, seeking always to do that which is best for all concerned. This is the surest way to attain peace and success in any kind of disagreement.

The sooner we all realize that we are working for God and not for men, the sooner we shall find peace, success, and happiness in all our affairs. Those who manage industry are managing the Father's business. It is their work to distribute God's substance to the best of their ability. Those who produce the physical necessities of life are the workers of God. They are not slaves nor are they drudgers. Like the managers, they too are about the Father's business. Both workers and managers are sons of God, fulfilling His divine purpose on earth. When we have learned to do all to the glory of God, we shall have found the key to successful working and joyous living. We shall know the joy that comes to those who are constantly going about the Father's business.

Is There a Sure Cure for Alcoholism?

ANNE HOWARD WATERS

MUCH HAS BEEN accomplished in public education on the subject of alcoholism. It has been pointed out that the alcoholic is mentally ill. An even more important point, however, is that the alcoholic needs spiritual healing; therein lies the only predication on which a lasting cure can be based.

From a psychiatric standpoint the alcoholic is one of the most difficult of patients to restore to normalcy for, like the drug addict and the criminal, he receives a kind of satisfaction, or pleasure, from his behavior. True, he may suffer "the morning after," but at the time of his drinking he finds release from tension, worry, a sense of inferiority, or any of the numerous neurotic ailments from which chronic alcoholism springs. Thus the psychiatrist claims that an alcoholic may not be cured until he feels the need of such a cure or has ceased to derive pleasure from his alcoholism.

If the alcoholic presents a difficult problem spiritually it is because he is hard to reach through direct approach. One of the outstanding characteristics of the alcoholic, whether he be a "social drinker" or an out-and-out drunkard, is his fear of spiritual contact. He avoids people, situations, and conversation dealing with God. Sometimes he scoffs; perhaps he hides behind an attitude of indifference or intolerance. Basically he senses his loss of contact with God and, like a lost child, is frightened.

The application of Truth principles with consistent, unwavering faith offers a positive answer to the problem. The Truth student does not depend on direct, or verbal, contact with the alcoholic. Instead he depends directly on God, from whom all health, mental and physical, flows in abundance. The Christ Spirit within the Truth student speaks to the Christ Spirit within the unfortunate victim —mightily, effectively, and unequivocally—to inaugurate the program of rehabilitation from within.

Lest this seem theoretical, I should like to relate an actual case history in which a young man was healed of alcoholism through the application of Truth principles—and to assure you that this case history is but one of a dozen I could cite. We shall call our alcoholic "Bob."

Bob had a beautiful, intelligent, loving wife and two small children. He had come to our company directly from college, an eager, ambitious youth. His natural charm and good nature, plus hard work and enthusiasm, advanced him rapidly until he had an excellent sales position. It was an accepted belief that he would one day be sales manager.

His drinking started unobtrusively. At first it was merely a pre-luncheon highball with a customer.

Then, as tension and pressure increased during the early war years when his selling became more a matter of detail work on defense accounts and his territory increased because of curtailed personnel, Bob began to take two or three drinks at the end of the day "to relax," he explained.

Within two years he was an out-and-out alcoholic —to everyone but himself. "More contracts are signed in bars than in the White House!" he argued belligerently when the boss suggested he "take it easy." It was not too long until he was to discover that contracts could be lost in bars too—when a man talks too loudly and too much, with too little attention to the courtesies and kindnesses that build friendships.

"It looks pretty hopeless," the boss remarked when we discussed Bob's situation. "All the authorities on alcoholism admit you can't do anything until or unless the person realizes he needs help. I've talked to Bob. He simply refuses to admit he drinks too much. It looks like I'm going to have to let him go, and I hate to. Ellen's a wonderful girl—and those two sweet kids of his . . ."

"Let me see what I can do," I suggested.

The boss shook his head. "You're licked before you start. He won't even talk to you—sober, that is. And if you run into him when he's drinking— well, he can get awfully abusive."

"I'm not going to talk to Bob—for a while anyway." I explained a little of my idea.

The boss agreed, reluctantly. "O. K. Sounds like pure theory to me—but go ahead."

Ellen, Bob's wife, was the starting point. I laid the facts before her as gently as I could. Her face was tight and hurt as she told her side of the story. It was an old, pathetic tale: incidents of public humiliation, of verbal and even physical abuse.

"It's hopeless," she said tiredly. "I've scolded and nagged until I feel like a fishwife. He says nobody is going to tell him what he may or may not do. I know he loves the children and me. You couldn't find a sweeter, more considerate husband—when he isn't drinking. But the problem is just bigger than he is!"

"Would you be willing to try an experiment?" I asked.

"I'll try anything—do anything!"

"Do you believe in God, in His power and ability to help Bob?"

Her shoulders slumped. "Oh—that! Of course I do—only—well, Bob just snorts when anybody mentions religion. It's part of the change in him."

"You're not going to speak to Bob about it in the accepted sense of the word," I countered. "The Christ Spirit within you will speak to the Christ Spirit within him—silently, frequently, and affirmatively."

Ellen listened skeptically but attentively as I outlined the plan. As we progressed she saw its unalterable logic. Here is how it worked:

Each morning when Ellen awakened she looked at Bob and said silently: *"The Christ Spirit within you gives you abundant health and wholeness, confidence, enthusiasm, and strength."* As she kissed Bob good-by she silently blessed him: *"God bless you. His limitless good infolds you every minute of this day."* During the day when she found her thoughts straying to the "worry-line" she reiterated the blessing and affirmed: *"The Christ Spirit within you, Bob, manifests itself in goodness."*

At the very outset Ellen realized the importance of her own mental attitude. When a thought picture of Bob staggering up the path occurred to her she conscientiously replaced it with one of him clear-eyed and smiling, bending to scoop one of the children up in his arms. When his unkind words, spoken in a moment of alcoholic rage, returned to haunt her, she recalled the many gentle, comforting experiences they had shared.

There was a third part of the program. By her own admission Ellen had scolded and nagged. This practice was replaced, not by mere tolerance but by active, positive love. She met Bob at the door in a clean, crisp dress. Her welcoming kiss was genuine and loving. She laid out fresh linen and clean towels for his evening shower, a ritual he had too frequently forgotten of late. The dinner table was set attractively. She served the foods Bob particularly enjoyed. She taught the children to bring him the evening paper and his slippers as part of the new regime. It was not Bob, the alcoholic, that Ellen treated as such a loved and honored guest in their home, but the Christ Spirit in Bob, whose manifestation she affirmed with almost every breath.

"You are closest to Bob," I explained to Ellen, "but you are not alone in your affirmations and prayers. I shall be making them with you, and so will at least two other Truth students in the office who are Bob's friends."

Bob's recovery was not immediate. Nor was Ellen's own demonstration perfect or consistent at first. However, there was a recognizable improvement in two weeks. The first month there were "slips"—nights when Bob's staggering footsteps made it difficult for Ellen to continue her blessings and affirmations—but she held fast. At the end of the month, the boss, noticing an improvement in Bob, suggested that he take a vacation. "I'll lend you my own mountain cabin," the boss added.

Ellen left the children with her mother so she could accompany her husband. "I felt that those two weeks were a direct gift from God," she told me later. "It gave both of us the opportunities we needed. It took Bob away from the temptations of his daily associates and it gave me the peace of mind I needed to strengthen my faith."

A year later, after she was sure of his complete recovery, Ellen told her husband how the healing had been accomplished.

"I'll never be able to put into words what I

felt, even that first week," Bob, now a Truth student himself, told me not long ago. "I felt more relaxed, more at peace. It seemed like something inside of me urged me to do little things I'd forgotten to do, like building a sandbox for the youngsters instead of spending Saturday with the boys. I'd pick up a bouquet for Ellen. I got the idea it'd be fun to take the family on a picnic after work. I began to feel important—maybe 'loved' is a better word. It was almost like having an invisible me along all the time. That other me was a swell guy, and I found myself trying to live up to him."

"How about the actual drinking, Bob?" I asked. "Was it much of a struggle to give that up?"

"That's the strangest part of it all," Bob replied. "Especially after Ellen and I went on the trip to the mountains, I just didn't feel like I wanted a drink." He grinned engagingly. "It'd make me a hero if I could say I 'sweated it out'—but actually I didn't. It got so liquor didn't taste good—made me a little nauseated. I remember accusing the bartender of selling me cheap whisky. No, I didn't have any more trouble leaving it alone than castor oil!"

The alcoholic is not God's stepchild. He has simply strayed from his normal contact with his Father. The Christ Spirit dwells within him, just as it does within us all. Thus there is no "hopeless" alcoholic *if even one person* speaks to that Christ Spirit consistently and with unwavering faith in its power to manifest itself.

Collecting Bills the Easy Way

LOWELL FILLMORE

RECENTLY a businessman brought his problem to me. A number of his customers owed him money and were not responding to his monthly statements and collection letters. His question was: Should he sue them, or could collections be made by Truth methods? As this same problem may be troubling others, I will give my thoughts concerning its solution.

Every problem can be solved by Truth methods because back of Truth is God, and we know that all things are possible with God.

Of course when any creditor undertakes to collect a difficult debt by means of the prayer method he must proceed in quite a different manner than he would if he were trying to collect the money by the usual methods. It would certainly seem out of place to bring suit to collect money after asking God to collect it.

God works through a universal divine law of justice. This law will adjust your financial affairs if you will conform to it. This law of divine justice must first be accepted as the collector's standard of dealing before it is applied to the debtors. The collector must attune his mental attitude to the law

73

of justice before he can successfully use it on
the other fellow. In fact, the principal work in
collecting an account must be done in one's own
mind. This may sound foolish and impractical to
one who is unaccustomed to depending on a higher
power than manmade law for help. Nevertheless
it is true that "the foolishness of God is wiser than
men; and the weakness of God is stronger than
men."

Under the divine law of justice your own comes
to you when you make the conditions right for receiving it. Justice cannot work properly in your
affairs so long as you have thoughts that impede
it, such as thoughts of condemnation of your debtor.
Condemnation and bitterness build up a wall between you and him. They actually make it difficult
for him to pay you. The debtor should be set at
liberty to act freely under the law of justice.

Your wholehearted silent blessing will help to
liberate him. By blessing him and realizing that you
and he are both working under the divine law of
justice you will relieve him of the pressure of doubts
and hard feelings and open a way for the law
of justice to function in your mutual affairs. You
can free him from the atmosphere of depression that
he may be laboring under, and which may be pre-
venting him from paying you. Through your thoughts
you can help him to find a way to obtain money to
pay you.

"Molasses will catch more flies than vinegar."

The right kind of thoughts and words will likewise accomplish better results than negative, critical, condemning words and thoughts. Therefore, the first thing to do to collect a hard account is to begin setting yourself free from thoughts of condemnation, lack, and doubt, and to continue to do so until you have a perfectly good friendly feeling toward your debtor. After that, practice realizing that your supply is coming from the one inexhaustible Source. This realization will prosper your business and open the way for better collections.

Your business will increase in volume and earnings when you are able wholeheartedly to understand that all of your success comes from God, and not from customers but through customers. This realization entered into many times a day will keep the channel of your supply open, and your business will flow freely and naturally to you through many men's hands.

By realizing that God is your supply you can change the whole mental atmosphere of your office so that your business associates and your environment will radiate prosperity. All coldness, resentment, doubt, and antagonism will be crowded out by this realization of God's omnipresence. What if one or two of your debtors do not pay their bills? God will prosper you in other ways. But I am confident that if you will bring your affairs under the divine law and will bless your debtors every day they will all pay eventually.

Take this thought for yourself: *"My justice comes from the Lord, and I am prospered in all my ways."* Then hold the same thought for your debtor, saying: *"Your justice comes from the Lord, and you are prospered in all your ways."* Set him free in God's love, erasing from your mind every harsh thought against him. In other words, make it easy for him to pay you, and he will pay you.

What Is a Christian Businessman?

FRANCIS J. GABLE

W E HEAR A great deal about Christian businessmen. We hear of men who are applying Christianity in their business affairs, as if such an application were something new. Is it reasonable to ask: What is a Christian businessman? Have we not had Christian businessmen for years, or has something new been developed out of all the former teachings that we have heard concerning the Christ?

Thus far in world affairs, so-called Christian people have been content to base their activities on the question: What would Jesus do? They ask themselves what they should do to act as Jesus might act under any given circumstance. They hang the teachings of Jesus on their walls and regard them as a code of ethics or as rules of conduct by which they should govern their ordinary activities. When the impulse to do a certain thing arises within them they look at their ethical code to see whether or not they should do that thing, and they are governed by what the rules tell them. But the teachings of Jesus constitute more than a code of ethics. There is a livingness about them that operates within a man and may become the dominating power of his life. We often see a stone lying by the side of the road. Nearby is a flowering plant, and as we look at the two objects we say to ourself that one is a living thing and the other is dead, inert. A chemist might take the stone and the plant to his laboratory and by analysis find that the same elements exist in both; the difference between them, in our eyes, is occasioned by the manifest presence in one of the principle that we call life. The same difference exists in the recognition of Christianity by different people. To some it is an outer thing; to others it is a living, breathing, indwelling presence.

It is tremendously important that the world begin to consider why Jesus did or did not do certain things. Jesus taught that the underlying motives of a man are what really count. He said that it is what comes out of the heart that governs what a man is. He taught an attitude of mind that is based on eternal principles; He did not pay so much attention to the external acts of an individual as He did to the attitude of mind that might make those acts possible. Most of His teachings are what might be called simple facts, yet they are eternal truths. They are not true because He said them but He said them because He knew them to be true.

A Christian businessman, in the highest sense of the word, is a man who recognizes the higher powers of man as Jesus taught them. He recognizes that these powers come from but one source, and he also recognizes that his outer life is an exact picture of the manner in which he uses these powers.

Jesus said: "If any man would go to law with thee, and take away thy coat, let him have thy cloak also." If any man goes to law with another and takes away his coat, the other is compelled to do that which is not according to his will. Yet as a child of God he has been endowed with the right of choice and in order to exercise that right he must be free to do that which he is not compelled to do. It is in the giving of the cloak or in the going of the second mile that man expresses himself as a free agent. He manifests a self-mastery of conditions that are essential to the highest attainment. The man today who declares that such a course is not practicable, that it would not work in business, offers a direct affront to the Christ. So great a teacher as Jesus would not promulgate an idea that was not practical, and His greatness is attested today by the influence that His life and His works have had and now have on the entire world.

Jesus also taught: "With what measure you mete, it shall be measured unto you." Many have considered that statement in the light of a possible barter and trade. Several hundred years later the same idea was announced to the world in its reference to physics, in the law that for every action there is an equal reaction; the mechanical world today uses this law in many, many ways. Jesus made His assertion because it was revealed to Him as being an eternal truth that was applicable to all activities of man and was not confined to physical things. The businessman of today who has made this law a part of his being gives out in service, in effort, and in efficiency, freely and liberally, and he knows that the same measure will be meted to him again, in good will and in profits.

A Christian businessman is one who tries to establish within himself the mind that is also in Christ Jesus. He recognizes that he is inherently divine and his highest effort is exerted toward manifesting in thought, in word, and in deed the divinity within him. His mind is open to receive the inspiration that comes to him from his higher self. His mind is as the mind of a little child, free from bias and prejudice, and ever reaching out to know more of the great things of life.

The Christian businessman radiates in his activities many qualities that distinguish him from the man who is not a Christian. The distinction may not always be apparent to the mind of the one who observes it, but it is very apparent to the intuition. By his radiations the Christian businessman creates about him and about his place of business an atmosphere that attracts people because of a sense of confidence that it inspires in them. The Christian businessman has an effect on his employees that stimulates them always to the highest endeavor and helps to develop in them the highest efficiency, morally, mentally, and physically. He reflects in his home and in his social affairs the same Christ qualities that he radiates in his business life and affairs.

Often the Christian businessman feels that he is stepping out on an untried road, because so few of his fellows have been operating by the high and lofty principle by which he operates. Yet he is not fearful of the results of his excursion into the untried, for he possesses an assurance that is based upon that which is unchangeable and eternal. His heart is filled with Christ love, and through his love he sees a perfect oneness established between himself and God, between himself and all men.

Such is the typical Christian businesssman.

The Power of Faith

HAROLD S. KAHM

HOW CAN FAITH, which is an intangible, invisible thing, alter or influence conditions that we call material and real?

You might as well ask how electricity, which no man has ever actually seen, can hurl a train over a mountain at sixty miles an hour. You might as well say that the wind, which is formless and invisible, could not possibly destroy a building made of heavy wood and iron, solidly anchored to a firm foundation. But this would be denying the roaring power of a tornado.

You cannot see the air you breathe, but you cannot live for five minutes without it. So in this respect you, as a very real and physical object, materially speaking, depend for your very existence on something that is intangible and invisible to you. And how hard it doubtless is for you to realize that this same intangible atmosphere is pressing against you at the rate of nearly fifteen pounds to the square inch. And what is lighter than air? Surely this defies the reasoning power of the average man.

If you consider this book—a material object—in the light of modern science you will know that what you are now holding in your hand is a collection of

82

invisible atoms, molecules, and electrons, all possessing enormous physical energy.

You, no more nor less than the book, and the seat in which you may be sitting, are composed of these same violently active atoms, molecules, and electrons. As a matter of fact, you physically are no more than a collection of atoms, molecules, and electrons in the shape of you.

Faith is no more visible than electricity, or a hurricane, or the air we live in and breathe, or the molecules and atoms that compose every animate and inanimate object in the universe. But there is no greater force available to mankind.

God too is invisible. God is the power that created the universe, that keeps atoms and electrons in motion, keeps your heart beating, the sun shining, the grass growing. God is the source of all power. The word *God* is unimportant in itself; it is a symbol of the mysterious power that created and controls the world and everything in the world. If you doubt this, your very ability to doubt—or to think—comes from the same mysterious source. It is a circle; there is no escape. If you are a skeptic concerning everything involving the word *God,* call this mysterious power the x quantity in the scientific manner. If you are a Mohammedan, call it Allah. You can change the name to suit your fancy, but you cannot alter the gigantic fact. It is like the law of gravitation. You can call it by any other name, but you must adjust yourself to it, abide by its rules, or be destroyed.

The enormous, invisible power of God is within you. Without it you can do nothing. With it you can do anything, everything.

The key to this power is faith.

Now let's get down to cases. You separate the material world from the invisible quality of God and faith. This, alas, is the commonest human error. We live actually in a wholly mental world, and nothing exists save in our mental conception of it—absolutely nothing! The brain alone gives reality. Sight, sound, touch, taste, smell—these senses are not physical but mental in that they are all located in the brain, in the consciousness. You taste with your mind rather than with your tongue; you are reading this with your mind rather than with your eyes. The body and senses are mere adjuncts of the mind, and they are not even necessary adjuncts. Your five senses can function just as effectively in the course of a dream—or a nightmare—as they can during your waking hours. A dream or a nightmare can be and often is as vivid as "reality."

Reality is as mysterious and intangible as the air we breathe. And that invisible air is a part of reality. It is a material object just as much as the house you live in. It is well to remember this when you ask, "How can faith, which is invisible and intangible, change or influence something that is real and material?"

How does faith really operate to change what we call reality? We have a number of clues, but the final fact is, like the universe itself, shrouded in divine mystery. But of this we can be sure: the power of faith is no more mysterious than the power of gravitation—which is invisible—or of electricity —which is invisible—or of radium, which is likewise invisible. The power that transmits the sound from a radio broadcasting station to you is invisible. The mightiest forces known to man are intangible, invisible powers. The strongest of these is faith.

Faith can and does move mountains even in the most literal sense. Power shovels are employed probably, but it is faith that provides the basic flow of power. First there is the idea of moving a mountain in the mind of some man who has faith that he can bring it about, who calmly believes that it can and will be done. Then there is the engineer who himself must believe it can be done. One engineer, offered the job, may have no faith in this direction. He says, "It's impossible," and offers an impressive list of technical reasons to prove how utterly impossible it is. Another engineer, undismayed by the apparent obstacles, says, "It's a big job, but I can do it." Then he does it because he knows he can do it. And he may do it without so much as touching the mountain with his hand; he causes it to be done. The power shovels and the laborers who individually believe they don't have a chance to amount to much in this world do all the physical work.

The story of human progress is a history of faith. Almost every great inventor and scientist in the world was told, "It can't be done." The technical obstacles were insurmountable save by one means alone: determined faith. The world scoffed at the Wright brothers; it was believed to be utterly impossible for man to fly. Scientists "proved" it to be impossible. Even such a great man as Alexander Graham Bell (who had believed in the telephone) accepted their verdict. Bell had no faith in flying. But the Wright brothers believed they could fly. Fly they did.

God is in everything, in every atom; faith in anything is actually faith in God. You have never seen or heard of a successful man in any walk of life who didn't possess some kind of strong faith: faith in his ideas, faith in his knowledge, faith in his luck, faith in a circumstance, faith in something. When you are repeatedly told that a person cannot succeed in any endeavor without self-confidence you are actually hearing a testimony to the power of faith, while the absence of positive faith results in failure.

Confidence in oneself is just what? It is confidence in the mysterious, divine force that is within one, the force that is individuality, source of personal power, the force that keeps the brain functioning, sends ideas and directs efforts.

If every successful man has faith—and you will find it impossible to find one who doesn't have it in one form or another—then by the same token the man who lacks positive faith is a failure. Faith is either good or bad, positive or negative; it is impossible to exist with entire lack of faith; you continually believe something. Faith is what you believe in your heart. Your beliefs have been conditioned by your education, by your parents and friends, and by what you see and hear and read. You judge the world by these things and shape your belief according to your judgment.

Before the Wright brothers, men saw for themselves, heard, and tested the principle that it was utterly impossible for men to fly. So that is what they believed, and flying for them was consequently impossible. Jesus said clearly, "Judge not, lest ye be judged." When you judge, on the basis of the visible, material things, you are reckoning without the most powerful forces extant. Your belief, your faith, is affected and defiled; you thus become a victim of this judgment.

The average man begins a new undertaking, whether in business, love, or health, by judging. He judges distances, obstacles, and difficulties, and by acknowledging their existence gives them power to oppose him. He believes in them. He becomes a victim of his own judgment. The man who succeeds is always one who refuses to believe in defeat. What he believes in either case will determine his destiny.

Nor is it possible to judge how God will be able to alter the material facts or conditions that seem to oppose one. It is foolish indeed to say to oneself, "I can't do anything about this, so how can God?"

Leave that to God. Said Jesus, "To God all things are possible" and again "To God nothing is impossible" and "I have ways ye know not of."

Faith is the single means to the help of God. For God is the source of all supply, all power, and there is no other in all the world. Jesus taught that the key to this enormous power is faith. There is nothing unreal about this. Every great man in the history of the world has demonstrated it in one way or another.

Faith is the biggest thing on earth.

Praying Wives

MARGARET HARFIELD

THERE ARE SOME very successful men who believe that prayer has had no part in making them the prosperous, contented citizens that they are. I think they may be mistaken.

Recently on the city street I was stopped by a woman. There was something familiar about her, and still I thought she was no one I knew. When she told me her name I was amazed. I did know her but had failed to recognize her because of the improvement in her appearance. Partly because I realized that my show of amazement was rude and partly because I desired to learn more about her, I asked her to lunch with me.

At lunch that day, she happily told me what had caused the change in her and in her entire world. She was not the same person she had been; there was no reason for her to look the same.

"And the whole thing," she said with a smile, "is an answer to my prayers for my husband's success. He was working such long hours for so small a wage—you remember how little we had."

I expressed my delight in her progress and asked her if she would mind telling me all about it.

"Mind!" She was so full of radiant enthusiasm

89

that she fairly shone; my imagination could not quite bring into focus the former mousy little woman who had appeared to me always as rather frightened and unfriendly. "Indeed I don't mind. It is not a long story; that is, it won't take many words to tell it to you. But it has taken us so far away from the past that those years seem unreal to us now.

"It wasn't any certain creed that taught me how to pray. It was my desperation at our situation and my earnest desire to help lift my husband to his right place in the world. Perhaps that is why everything has worked out so beautifully. For I can honestly say that the prayer was not selfish. I was praying for his success.

"I was familiar with Jesus' words, 'When thou prayest, enter into thy closet, and when thou hast shut thy door, pray to thy Father which is in secret.' One night I literally went into our clothes closet and shut the door. I felt completely alone with God. I asked Him to give my husband his right work. I pledged myself to God to do all that I could to further my husband's good and pledged myself to go anywhere and do anything that God directed. And I thanked Him that He had heard me and was working everything out right. Each day I prayed and constantly I thanked God. 'I shall love living in a city or I shall love living in the country,' I promised. 'Dear God, I will be happy wherever You send us.'

"In three weeks my husband heard of a place where he might find better work in a city not far away. He mentioned it to me, and although he did nothing about it in the outer, I began to pray about it. Two weeks after that he came home in the middle of the morning and said: 'I've just had a call from the man in the city I told you about. A salesman told him about me, and he wants me to come to work right away. What do you think?' I said, 'Call him and tell him you will come.'

"That was the beginning. Since then I have prayed and prayed.

"My husband kept that work for a time. Then he came home one night and said that he had quit. There was a dishonest situation there. While it did not concern him particularly, he would no longer stay. This was a surprise to me, but I knew in my heart that prayer was bringing him to a better position.

"I had learned some Truth principles by then and I affirmed over and over lovingly and joyously, *'My husband is now in his right place, doing his perfect work.'* And I had faith. I didn't worry for a minute. After resting a week, he applied at three places in one day. That night the owner of the place he had his heart set on called and asked him to come to work the next morning. The next day I received two telephone calls telling me that he had been selected to fill the other positions for which he had applied. 'Good measure, pressed down . . . running over!'

"My husband is now in charge of many men and has a position that entails great responsibility. He is earning a high salary. He loves his work, is completely happy in it. He has bought three pieces of property and he has acquired a wonderful prosperity consciousness.

"Should I slow down in my praying now? No! My husband knows now that I am praying about his business and his success. And he has come to depend on my help. I'm certain he prays in his own way, but he also has much faith in my prayers for him.

"When an opportunity for a good investment comes along, he asks, 'Is this rather sudden?' My answer is something like this, 'No, it came in order; I've been expecting it.' He never questions the answers to my prayers any more, and I know that his faith is placed not in me but in God, who is the answer to our every need."

As she finished I wondered why we all forget so often that Jesus said we are to come in faith as little children. Successful men are not the only ones who become smug and feel that they have won a triumph alone; we all forget at times that the God who is our Creator is also our sustainer.

Perhaps the reason why men often lose sight of the necessity of prayer in their business is that they are so completely occupied with the outer tasks that are theirs. They do not have the time, it seems, to study the Bible and to meditate and pray. They may not be reminded by their wives that prayer is doing its perfect work in their careers, for wives may hesitate to mention such matters to their husbands.

Each praying wife who has learned something of Truth knows that her husband's mental attitude has much to do with the success of his business. She knows that he can have a blind faith that will help sometimes in a pinch. She knows that often he hits on the law and works with it for a while and says he has had a tremendous streak of luck. But she knows too that success in business or in anything else must have a firm foundation if it is to last and give joy in the accomplishment. The praying wife knows that faith, love, will to do, and power to accomplish make up this firm foundation —and are found only in the spiritual realm, which can be reached by prayer.

Many a successful man realizes the part that his wife has played in his career through her prayers—and thanks her for it. And it may be that many a man who believes that he has climbed the heights alone has given himself too much credit. Investigation might show that his wife has been doing some powerful praying about him and his business; that he, his wife, and God have been partners in business for many years.

Learning the Other Fellow's Language

CHARLES HENRY MACKINTOSH

I THINK THE HARDEST TASK I ever had to tackle was that of turning myself inside out, from my natural state as a poet and an introvert, into —of all things—a public speaker! Since other readers of this magazine may have a similar ordeal thrust upon them at practically any moment, they may as well profit by my experience.

It came upon me as a shocking surprise. I had not been able to break away from my advertising service business to go with the gang to the district conference of the Rotary clubs of my district of Rotary International, but they came back with the ultimatum that I was the newly elected district governor!

There was an implicit obligation to go to every Rotary club in the district and deliver an official oration.

The only public "speeches" I had consciously delivered up to that time had been "readings" rather than speeches, for I wrote them out and read them when I couldn't get out of speechmaking entirely. My articles in The Rotarian had given the gang the idea that I might make a good governor; but I knew I couldn't go around the district reading

articles. I would have to learn—and fast—to talk on
my feet!

I don't recall just how many wakeful nights I
spent before it came to me that I had been wholly
mistaken in thinking I had no real previous experience as a public speaker. What had I been doing
to prospects for white space in the Star, and to my
own clients for advertising service, if not making
public speeches to them?

After all, normal speaking is all public speaking, for only those who have lived alone too long
talk to themselves. The rest of us almost never talk
at all except to an audience, and if the nature of our
need to talk at all has included convincing the other
fellow that he should do something, why, what finer
practice in the art of effective public speaking could
one need or hope to get than just that?

All of us who gain any sort of lasting success
in selling do so because we have taught ourselves
to talk in the language of the other fellow instead
of in terms of our own ideas, opinions, prejudices,
and interests. This language of the other fellow is
also the language of effective public speaking.

It is a foreign language to most of us, and so we
have to learn it just as we would have to learn any
other foreign language, first thinking in our own
language and then deliberately and consciously
translating every word and idea into that other
language. For example, in France we may frame
the thought, "Where's the nearest post office?" but

before we can hope to have the gendarme understand and direct us, we shall have to turn the thought into this: "Où est le bureau de poste le plus proche?"

Just so our natural impulse may be to say to a neighbor, in the language of our own prevailing interest in the matter: "I do hope it doesn't rain this morning! I forgot my umbrella." If we wish to translate that thought into his language, however, we shall have to change the primary approach and almost every word: "A good soaking rain about now would be the salvation of this lawn of yours; and it looks as if you are going to get it!" You may then go on to borrow his umbrella.

This is the real language of effective public speaking; not oratory, not rhetoric, but the language of the other fellow. Rhetoric has its place, and so do eloquent gestures have their place; but one can make an effective public speech without either—which one cannot possibly do without using the language of the other fellow.

As Paul wrote in the 13th chapter of I Corinthians, "Though I speak with the tongues of men and of angels, and have not charity, I am become *as* sounding brass, or a tinkling cymbal." And he used the Greek word, *agape* for "charity," implying compassion, which is the ability to feel with others.

It is the cultivated ability to feel with others, to put oneself in their place and see any proposition in terms of their interests and prejudices rather than in "normal" terms of one's own, that distinguishes the effective public speaker.

Paul made this type of approach to the people of Athens who were, he knew, highly skeptical on the subject of new religions. He began by reminding them that they had already raised in their own City-State an altar to "AN UNKNOWN GOD," and it was this unknown God that he proposed to make known to them.

Again, to the much smaller but even more menacing audience he faced when he had been haled before King Agrippa, he used the same approach. "I think myself happy, king Agrippa," he began, "because . . . *I know* thee to be expert in all customs and questions which are among the Jews." At the end of this speech, remember, Agrippa said to Festus, "This man might have been set at liberty, if he had not appealed unto Cæsar."

Effective public speaking may usually be known and judged by the fact that it leads to favorable action, even if the action be nothing more than prolonged applause. It leads the members of the Parent-Teacher Association to put themselves on record in the public press in favor of higher pay for more teachers. In wartime it makes patriotic bond buyers buy more bonds than they had intended to buy. It makes the charitable "give till it really hurts." It made King Agrippa want to release Paul. All this it does because it interprets the thing to be done in terms of the interests of those who must do it, if it is to be done at all, speaking always and only in the language of the other fellow.

Deliberately to acquire, through constant practice in the ordinary conversations of every day, the habit of translating into the language of the other fellow our own naturally self-centered reactions to events, people, and things, not only is sound practice in salesmanship and in public speaking but it may also be seen as a means to constant advancement in the very art of living itself. For the art of living is the art of learning to live with others; it is Paul's art of compassion, of feeling with others —or learning the other fellow's language.

The Obnoxious Buyer

RUSSELL W. LAKE

THIS IS AN ACCOUNT of my personal experience with the inexorable law of cause and effect—and recognition that the right cause brings the right effect. I had a lesson to learn before I realized the true foundation of human relationships.

My justification for writing about myself is that probably my attitude and my experiences are common to those of a great many other persons, and therefore contain a common lesson. We all must climb to the same plateau of understanding before we can live without continual struggle seasoned with worry.

I had been a salesman for years, traveling the State of Kansas. I prided myself on the fact that I worked hard and was a pretty good salesman. During those years I made a fair living for myself and family but I never reached the point where I felt that I could relax even for an hour. Had to keep going, you know, to get the business before someone else got in ahead of me.

Working under conditions like these is bound to pile up dark mountains of worry and resentment. In the shadow of these mountains a person worries if he has a bad week's business, or even one unsatisfactory day. He resents almost everything that is not quite to his liking. He considers his accounts unreasonable and obstinate if they refuse to buy as much as he thinks they should. He considers them poor businessmen. He resents the fact that his line does not have all the selling features his competitors have. He resents the inclement weather that makes it hard for him to work. He resents.

I went through all this. I had one buyer especially whom I considered inordinately tough. He was the buyer for a large store in Wichita, and I always felt that his position had gone to his head. If the account had not been so large, I would have passed him up completely, feeling that life was too short to put up with a fellow like that. But for selfish reasons, I continued to call on him and of course continued to snarl inwardly at his lack of enthusiasm for me and my line.

He was an extremely cold person and very gruff. He was thin and tall and he had bushy black eyebrows over deep-set eyes that always seemed to glare. He hardly deigned to look up from his work when a salesman was ushered in. Most buyers at least attempted to hold a conversation with me, but not he. About the only thing he would say was "No," except on rare occasions when he would say a whole sentence: "I don't need any." He never gave a salesman a chance to make a whole presentation. On very rare occasions, he would interrupt me almost before I got started and would call a saleswoman from her department. He would ask her to bring her inventory sheets and then would instruct her to order enough goods to bring her total up to the standard inventory. The ordering would take place in his office. Salesmen were not allowed to talk to the women in the department. All instruction in methods of resale must be done in his office. He was a thorn in the side of every salesman who called on him.

I struggled along with him and with all the others for years. It seems strange now that anyone could be so ignorant as I was about human relations, especially when I thought I knew considerable about the subject. I knew and believed that God is everywhere present. If you had asked me I would have answered: "Certainly, He is present in all things animate and inanimate, in the air about us and in the sky above and the earth beneath. He guides and directs all the stars and planets, maintaining their proper equilibrium and He will guide you and me if we but give Him the opportunity." But of course that had nothing to do with business! It never occurred to me to apply it to my stingy buyers.

I believe that divine wisdom is constantly trying to send us messages from within ourself. If we allow the messages to get through to our consciousness, we are directed into the right channels, not only of action but also of mental attitude.

One day I was in the office of the Wichita buyer and I was thinking what an outstanding degree of "orneriness" he possessed. I will not say I hated him; I merely considered him the most pigheaded, obstinate, and thoroughly unlikeable person I had ever met.

Suddenly the strange thought flashed into my mind that I was not talking to this man; I was talking to God in him. This buyer was a spiritually perfect individual, metaphysically speaking. Any outward appearance of undesirable personality did not truly portray the inward man. Since God is omnipresent He must be active within this buyer. It was only my own conceit that could lead me to believe that God was within me and not in him.

I actually felt humble. I began to bless the buyer. I blessed the divinity that moved within him. Before my eyes he changed from an obnoxious individual to a rather nice fellow. In the years I had called on him I had never seen him smile, but now I noticed the crinkles at the corners of his eyes that could easily have come from laughter. I worked hard on the idea that I had misjudged him.

There was no miraculous change in his attitude. He continued to fuss with papers on his desk while I talked about my product, but I did not feel the same resentment toward him that I always had felt before.

He did not buy. Perhaps I blessed him with reservations in spite of myself; or perhaps it was best for him that he not buy that trip. I do not know.

If he never had bought from me again I always would have felt I owed him a great deal nevertheless. From that day on I blessed each of my accounts and tried to realize that the buyers were not the mulish persons I always had considered them but were in fact divine. If my sales volume had not increased, I still would have gained much from my new understanding because I later awoke to the fact that I no longer worried about business.

My sales increased. They grew larger so gradually and so naturally that for a time I did not realize what was happening. My buyers became more friendly and greeted me with genuine welcome instead of the preoccupied handshake. This did not happen overnight but was the result of a gradual change in my selling methods. Instead of thinking of a sale as so many dollars of volume and so many dollars of commissions, I came to evaluate it from a broader aspect. If my selling operations were to be guided by Spirit within me and were to take into account Spirit within the buyer, surely there could be nothing but good resulting from each transaction. This counted out all high-pressure selling, all questionable methods, all overstocking of buyers. Formerly this would have smacked of weak-kneed selling, a method bound to bring on loss of business, slow starvation, and probably separation of me from my job.

I even began to feel a sense of comradeship with

my competitors' salesmen. There was no need for me to rush from one buyer to the next and from one town to the next in order to get the business before a competitor did. Surely there was enough for all of us. To believe that there was any lack of good was to deny the largesse of God. To feel, as I always had, that every order I sold was that much business taken away from a competitor was to believe in limited supply. Intellectually I had subscribed to the Truth that God's supply is unlimited, that all who call on Him receive ample measure. Now for the first time I put my belief to practical work. Good results were forthcoming for me throughout my territory.

In my contact with many of my customers there always had been a clash of purpose and an undercurrent of argument. It was the salesman-buyer attitude in which the salesman attempts to high-pressure a reluctant buyer. Too many salesmen feel they are at cross-purposes with their customers, and their customers feel the same way.

I believe we salesmen are misnamed. We are not men who sell; instead we are or should be men who provide a source of profit to our accounts. We ought to be renamed business counselors, because our job is to supply expert advice pertaining to the proper merchandising and resale of our particular product. When we fulfill our purpose we become channels through which God works to provide more good for our buyers.

All of us in business, whether we are selling at wholesale or retail or holding a non-selling position, should consider ourselves as channels through which good flows to the other fellow. When we take this attitude an even greater measure of good flows right back to us—but we can at least try to give more than we receive.

It was several months after I changed my attitude that the tough Wichita buyer one day suddenly dropped his pencil, leaned back in his chair, and began to talk to me. We talked for an hour or more. He said nothing about any change in my attitude or in his. It was as though I had dropped in on an old friend for a chat. From that time on, I enjoyed immensely my calls at his store, and our business was mutually profitable. A long time later I learned from him that he had developed a stiff pose toward salesmen because he had lost a very excellent position through being too "easy" a buyer. He blamed salesmen for overstocking him.

Perhaps some men in business have not had to go through what I did. Perhaps they have realized at once their true position in the scheme of creation and proceeded without the selfishness I exhibited. If such is the case they are fortunate because they have saved themselves a great deal of worry, a great deal of buffeting, and a very great deal of resentment.

I no longer am traveling the State of Kansas but I have carried the lesson with me. When I meet a person who seems to me to have a warped personality or an unpleasant demeanor, I try to remember that I am not looking at the man himself; I am seeing only the external of him like the cover of a book. The true man underneath lives and moves and has his being in God, just as the rest of us do. Spirit works within him to give him aspirations and abilities and the opportunity for a finer and fuller life. Such a man deserves our help, not contumely; love, not sarcasm. Our source is no more divine than his. It is the utmost of conceit to believe otherwise.

This principle applies to all our dealings with other persons, whether in business or out of it. We would serve our own purposes more fully if we would realize that God works in the other fellow too; that divine wisdom is his; that we have no right to judge that which is made of God.

When another person seems to be objectionable to us we do well to remember that his exterior is merely a mask that clothes the true man beneath; that Spirit is operating patiently to remove the mask from him as from ourselves in order to reveal the glorious person that is at the source of all of us. When we contact Spirit within him, we form a solid bridge that immediately becomes crowded with good flowing back and forth.

God's love is spread equally over all humanity, even to the least of His children. Let us all remember this.

Competition Is Foolish

MAURICE SMITH

FOR MANY YEARS I accepted competition as being a part of the American way of life. I operated my small business on a strictly competitive basis. The fact that I was competing with others for contracts had more effect on my estimating than the true value of the work to be done. As a result I quite often "stuck my neck out" and found myself doing work at a very low margin of profit. The volume was good, but the net profits were not in keeping with the amount of work done.

I found competition a hard taskmaster. It meant having very little time for myself or my family, spending most of my evenings and holidays with my nose to the grindstone. The ability to relax and enjoy myself had almost become a lost art. This eventually resulted in a physical breakdown, in which I was forced by nature to rest and take it easy—by no means an easy thing to do. For years I had lived by the sword of competition and I continued to fret about all the business my competitors were beating me out of.

I might very easily have been felled by this sword of competition that I had lived by so long, had it not been for an old friend who came to visit me one day. She tactfully started me to thinking about applying spiritual methods to the solution of my problems, especially business problems.

Being the type who has to be shown, I spent many months in gaining a full realization of the mighty power of these methods. With a better understanding came the knowledge that my misfortune was truly a blessing in disguise, as it gave me ample time to study the literature of practical Christianity. As time passed I began to see where I had erred.

By concentrating on competition I had made it a reality in my affairs. I had created my Old Man of the Sea and carried him around until I was exhausted. Recalling how some of my business associates had departed from the earth because of heart ailments and the like, I began to feel fortunate that my close adherence to competitive practices had resulted only in a physical breakdown.

With plenty of time on my hands I did a little research on competition. Webster describes it as "common strife for the same object." Sounds a little foolish, doesn't it, and inefficient?

Modern production methods have made it possible for a nation to provide more than the necessities of life for itself. Surely the all-providing Father never intended His children to engage in a mad scramble for His good. There are too many places in the Bible that guarantee abundance for this to be true.

In psychology I found competition closely associated with the fear of losing personal possessions. This fear stems from the recognition of two powers, good and evil, the all-providing Father on the one hand and a belief in lack and limitation on the other.

So I came to the conclusion that I had been missing the mark. As I was about to return to work, in my study periods I asked for guidance, resolving to ignore competition and to replace the idea with the spirit of co-operation. I changed my advertising to conform to this new policy, accentuating service, reliability, and quality.

Results were a little slow at first, but after a few months my net receipts were above what they had been during the old competitive days, and on not much more than half the work.

This gave me more time for my family, recreation, and study of the real basis of Christianity. Through these teachings I learned to relax; to let go and let God work in me; to build order and harmony into my affairs. Thus I became able to do better work in less time.

In the old days I would rise in the morning to face a battle for competitive survival. Now I greeted each new day with a sense of joyous expectancy. Through the years I had regarded my customer as a contestant in a three-sided game of wits, the other contestants of course being my competitor and myself. With the new attitude founded on Truth, I accepted each of my clients as an individual who needed my co-operation in bringing more good into his affairs.

This new type of customer I have attracted seldom asks for an estimate, being more concerned with quality, dependability, and service.

To the business people who have begun to tire from the strain of competition, I humbly offer this solution. The method will require faith, work, and co-operation, but a demonstration of good is sure to follow the use of it.

What Do You Really Want?

ELEANOR HUNTER

ONE OF THE MOST difficult things for worried, harassed people to understand is that what they really want is certain fundamental satisfactions instead of specific things.

Not a certain "deal"—but strong, accumulating success.

Not a certain house—but a perfect home.

Not a certain job—but satisfying work.

I have observed two cases recently. One has not yet been worked out while the other is complete, but they both show well what the real problem is and what is the right angle from which to approach it.

Let's take the uncompleted one first. This is the case of a woman—I shall call her Mrs. Biggs—who has a large and beautiful suburban property with several houses on it. The property is about to be taken by mortgage foreclosure, and she is struggling mightily to save it.

The one thing she insists on is that she must save it. It would seem that her heart would break if she does not save it, that the earth itself will slip out from under her feet and she will be stranded helpless, hopeless, and destitute. We can't blame her too much. Hers is a fairly common feeling. No matter what the problem, people are inclined to think it must be worked out in some specific way of their own devising.

I have told this woman that her "future" does not necessarily lie in her saving this property; that she must not outline her means of supply in specific terms. Instead she must stop and realize that what she really wants is security, plenty, a lovely home, her right place in the world, her right work, the overflowing sense of contentment, satisfaction, and the joy that such a condition would give her.

She pauses a few minutes in her grief and anxiety and admits, yes, these things are what she really wants. Then again she raises the tortured cry that these things can be achieved only by her saving this property.

I have told her that if she would forget the specific things and go back to the fundamentals of what she really desires she can rest serene in the complete and absolute knowledge that they are her divine inheritance. I have told her that they are "right here," present for her in the fullness of God's abundance and generosity and love for her; that she has a perfect right to ask for them and to expect them and know that she will get them; that indeed they are God's will for her, and nothing in heaven or earth can keep her from having them— nothing except her own insistent demand for this specific thing, which may not give her the fundamental satisfactions that are God's will for her.

I have told her that taking this stand of complete reliance in God's great goodness and might is sure to secure to her the property safe and sound and in a form that she can manage—if that is the best way for her to achieve the fundamentals which are her divine inheritance. I have explained that if the return of the property is not the answer, her trust in God's goodness will bring her the right answer, which can be an infinitely more satisfying one to her than retaining the property.

It is very difficult for her to see this. She can go just so far with me, but when it comes to relinquishing her mental hold on the property she is actually (though not consciously) insisting that she cannot trust God's wisdom to know what is right for her and her only possible good must come from saving this property—even if it is contrary to God's will!

Now let me describe the other case.

Mr. Jones is fifty. He had been an important executive in a big business in his city for twenty years. He was well known and had considerable standing not only in business but also in society. He was an expert in his line, but he knew no other business at all. He had a beautiful wife and two children, a son and a young daughter.

Mr. Jones knew nothing about Truth teachings; in fact he had no religious leaning at all. He had gone his own way more or less ruthlessly all his life, doing about what he pleased, cocksure that his way was the only one to be considered. Many people had suffered from his selfishness. He had hurt his wife cruelly by flagrantly taking up with another woman. His son had become estranged by this act. His daughter, whom he adored, suffered from the situation.

But his house of cards tumbled around him. As far as his business connection he had held so proudly all those years was concerned, he was "out" entirely. Some indiscreet investments failed, and he lost the bulk of his fortune. The beautiful home that he and his wife had built went to pay creditors. They had had to reduce their scale of living drastically; and because their position was so prominent, all of this was known to his associates.

These reverses began about a year before we met. When I saw him he was utterly despondent, cravenly self-reproachful, and contemplating suicide. He was altogether unable to see any answer to his needs but a restoration to his former glory.

I talked with him of fundamentals:

"Stop outlining the specific things you must have and get down to the fundamentals you want. Actually the specific things you did have did not give you what you really wanted, did they? You really wanted a loving, happy home, accord with your wife, the respect and affection of your son and daughter. You really want work to do that you can do so well that the doing will be a joy in itself. You want respect for yourself and your ability, not the old envy of your traditional position in the community. You want a life of satisfaction."

Yes, those were the things he wanted, he admitted. And then like Mrs. Biggs he kept going off on the disgrace and the shame it would be to him if he could not regain his former standing.

Helping him was not easy. As I said, he knew nothing about metaphysics, and God was only a word to him—a rather sappy word that weak people used. But during several lengthy meetings I was able to show him the very obvious reasonableness of Truth; how very obviously his experience was the fruit of his violations of divine law, and correspondingly, how his fulfilling the law would bring a different harvest. I showed him the poverty of his former condition in spite of all his money and his high standing: the poverty of his relationship with his wife; the poverty of years of no warm understanding between him and his son; the poverty of his little daughter's wordless fear and anxiety about conditions that she did not comprehend.

"You were not rich," I said to him. "You have lost nothing by this upheaval in your life. On the contrary, it was God's great goodness to you, sweeping away the falsities and making you turn to the good things you should be having as a glorious expression of God. You were running your life to ruin. God, acting through circumstances, showed His great love for you by making you change your life. Now if you can begin to see this and to recognize this

constant great power at your elbow guiding and
directing your every step, if you can know that your
right to the fundamentals of love and achievement
and prosperity and self-respect is a divine right,
you can stop your frenzied struggling, let go, and
trust that God will point out the rest of the way."

I suggested that he concentrate on one all-embrac-
ing idea. We selected *"Divine wisdom is guiding my
entire life,"* and he used it as a continual reminder
to himself.

Gradually his fundamental thoughts and words
began putting forth sprouts. He learned with amazement that his wife had completely forgiven him
for his past behavior and was wholeheartedly standing by him. (The other woman was out of the picture.) His son came home on leave. He and the
father had a conversation that resulted in the closest
understanding they had had in years and in the
son's expression of complete faith in his father.

But there still remained the matter of work and
income. He had taken a position with a company
engaged in a totally different kind of business, but
he was overcome at his own ineptness. "They're
only being kind to me in keeping me," he said. "I
don't know the business. I don't know what to do.
I go around all day trying to find something to do,
and I can't. I sit in conferences and don't know what
they are talking about. It's killing me. I couldn't
believe I could be so stupid and inefficient."

So we went to work on that. I said emphatically:

"It's ridiculous that you should be so lost. You simply can't tell me that you haven't your own place in the world, your right place, your right work and right income. You may not be in it any more than the piece of the jigsaw puzzle in the pile on the table is in its right place, but the piece of puzzle has its place, and it fits that place exactly without strain or struggle. So too, your perfect place exists, and it needs you as much as you need it. You are alive. Being alive, you are the center of the very activity of God. And God—the infinite activity of life itself—knows your right place and is able to bring you to it if you will stop fighting off your good through the blind action of your fears. You have your right place now, and nothing in heaven or earth can keep you out of it."

He looked at me, amazed that I could speak so positively. Then he asked almost timidly: "But what shall I do about it? How can I go about finding it?"

"Just do this one thing of getting a firm realization that your right place exists. When you are so sure of it that you no longer have any doubt about it, God will show you the steps to take; show you in such an unmistakable manner there can be no question in your mind. You'll know what to do, and there won't be any two ways about it."

About a month later he called me up and said, "You are now talking to the vice president of——." He named one of the largest concerns of its kind in the country, much larger than the one with which he had been connected all these years.

I laughed gleefully and said, "Tell me about it."

"Well," he said, "about ten days after our last talk the phone rang one evening. The caller was a man I hadn't seen in years—stopping in my city an hour between trains en route from California to New York. He told me this concern was looking for a man who knew the Middle West and had asked him about me. He suggested I get in touch with them. I did, and now I am their vice president."

God couldn't bring it to him? He must dash madly about, pleading with this one, trying "pull" through another? Well, God seemed to find him out! A telephone call to his own home, out of business hours, from a man he hadn't seen in years, who just "happened" to be stopping between trains!

God can always bring the right answer to anybody. It is not necessary to rush frantically hither and thither and feel an urgent demand to "do something" to save the situation. That very feeling holds off the answer. It is a repudiation of God, of God's wisdom, of God's knowledge of the situation, of God's loving will to do the good thing, of God's ability to do it. It is saying, "Well, if God won't do this for me I'll do it for myself—if it kills me." It is insisting on our own way whether right or not, very much like a stubborn child's insistence on playing in the poison-ivy patch his mother has urged him to keep out of.

If my friend Mrs. Biggs would tear her attention

away from the fixed idea of saving that property and turn in complete, wholehearted faith to the Truth that God does love her, does want the best for her, is more than willing to give her the best, and certainly has the power to do it; she could drop her strain, stop her tortured rushing about to find the necessary two or three thousand dollars. She could rest serene in the realization that something better is going to come out of this condition and even be eager to see what it will be.

How does she know that the property, with its taxes, its demand for care and attention, its failure to produce revenue, is not really her great burden? How does she know that the difficult situation she is in is not God's good way of taking her burden away and giving her the fundamental satisfactions she obviously has not been enjoying—else she wouldn't be losing the property—contentment and ease of living and abundance? Why can't she see that God knows where she is and if He wants her to have that property, He can seek her out with the solution that will give it to her without burden and strain? Why can't she see that if God gave her that beautiful place at one time in her life, He can give her a more beautiful place now?

It seems to me one of the greatest steps any student of Truth can take is to sit down and figure out his real desires.

A specific job—or completely satisfying work?
A specific "deal"—or ever-increasing success?

One's own way in an argument—or the harmonious solution of it?

None of us is wise enough to make his demands specific. We can't see far enough. Some demand or plan of ours may hold great harm around the corner of next week. It may not be big enough or comprehensive enough to meet God's will for us.

But if we think and ask in terms of fundamentals, the positive fundamentals of success, achievement, joy, abundance, congenial work, a perfect home, perfect love; we are sweeping away all restrictions and leaving the field wide open for all the good there is for us.

These things we can ask for on the most extravagant scale and know that we are not defying the will of God. They are the things God wants us to have to express the glory of His power through us. If we will put our demands on life in terms of these fundamentals, we won't need to be wishy-washy about asking. We don't need to be fearful of asking too much. We can ask with the utmost faith, which is the tool with which we carve our supply out of the infinite. We can know that, working in this manner, we are working with God, going with the mighty stream of life and its great forces, and that nothing is beyond their power. We shall then find results becoming manifest easily and gloriously and sit back in wonder and amazement at the fullness that God pours into our experience.

Thanksgiving for What?

GARDNER HUNTING

W E OFTEN think of gratitude as simply something we owe in return for good things that come to us. Actually it is a key with which we may unlock the closed door of consciousness and open our way into the house of plenty, where our heart's desire waits ready prepared for us to come and take it.

Thanksgiving is not the only key to this lock; but if you examine all the keys you will find a curious resemblance among them. Giving is a key to receiving; and there is certainly a likeness between giving and thanksgiving. Asking is a key to receiving; but all users of prayer come ultimately to find that thanksgiving is its most powerful form. Faith and trust are keys to open doors to our blessing, but the very essence of faith and trust is gratitude.

Let's ask ourselves a question: What do we mean by a blessing?

The way to get the most out of any questionnaire is to write down our answers before we look over to "page umpteen" to see what the book says, what the author says, what somebody else says. What we answer is the important thing. Let's be exact about it, define the blessing we want; no mere generalization

121

will do. The way to get what we want is to know what we want and then to understand that our desire is given us for the purpose of being fulfilled.

Maybe you don't believe this. Maybe you don't believe in God. Well, let's start where you are. Perhaps you think you don't believe in anything. If you will form the habit of giving thanks for everything that comes to you, you will come to believe in something. What label you put on that something when it becomes real to you does not matter in the least.

Are you ready to begin? Where will you begin? Exactly where you are. You can't begin anywhere else, can you, until you grow? And when you grow into some other position or condition or circumstance you will have a similar problem and want, in merely a new place or situation, until you solve that problem. When you learn to apply thanksgiving to your problems, you will find yourself in a new world; "Behold, I make all things new."

Let us suppose that you are sitting on a bootblack stand and a humble worker is shining your shoes. When he finishes you pay him of course. Perhaps you tip him. Very well. Thank him.

"Oh," you say, "payment is thanks enough. Anyhow a tip is the only thanks that will be appreciated. Besides, I thought thanksgiving meant thanking God."

It does. But can you thank one of the Creator's humblest creatures without thanking his Creator?

Payment is simply justice; tipping is a custom

against which there are sound arguments. But thanks, honest, sincere, genuine—that's the coin that buys heart's desires. Thank your bootblack.

His face may light up; it may not. If you mean what you say, that you are really grateful for his service, you will see a prompt result.

"But getting a shine is a trifling matter," you object. "I thought you were going to deal with important things."

You are beginning one of the most important things you will ever do: giving thanks where you are.

Perhaps you are reading a magazine article or a book you like that helps, instructs, inspires you. Say a thank-you. Silently, in prayer? Certainly. But also take your pen or your typewriter and write your thanks to the editor, the publisher, or the author. Your letter will reach any one or all of them if you send it in care of the publisher, whose name and address are on the publication. It isn't enough that you buy the book, subscribe for the magazine; you do that for yourself. Give thanks, a simple, plain expression of gratitude. Why? Because it will begin to solve your problem, whatever it is, right where you are. It will make you conscious of the reality of the blessing you desire; and consciousness of reality is what creates that reality for you.

Thank your friend for his kindness—for his companionship, for his thoughtfulness, for his friendship. Fulsome? Not if you are sincere. Of course thanks are not thanks unless they are genuine. Counterfeit won't buy you anything. Insincerity is insult.

Thank the salesman who waits on you. Thank your postman, your milkman, your newsboy. You think it is quite enough to pay them? Payment is for what you are receiving, not for what you hope to receive. You hope for the solution of your problem. Give thanks; you'll be surprised at the good results.

Thank the one who gives you a seat in bus, car, or train. Thank your cabdriver. Thank your wife for the good breakfast; your husband for the household money. Thank everybody for everything you receive or desire—not noisily or ostentatiously but just simply, honestly.

But suppose the service received is not good service. If you include thanks with your payment for it, it will improve—perhaps next time or the time after that. Sometimes the thank-you will touch the conscience of the worker, and he will improve his work there and then. But that is not your first purpose, to do something for him; your purpose is to solve your problem. Withholding thanks is like withholding water from your garden; the water does something for your flowers. Your thanks do something more than you can guess for the salesman, for your friend, for your wife, for your child, or for your newsboy. But the chief ultimate benefit is yours —yes, and the chief immediate benefit too. A thankful attitude is one of the greatest and most lasting benefits that will ever come to you.

Shall you be thankful for good news? Of course. For bad news? Yes. Often you do not know what news is good. There may be no bad news if you look on everything that comes to you as "a heavenly message"; on everybody who contacts you as a heavenly messenger—something, somebody to be thankful for; on disappointment as His appointment; on a closed door simply as a road sign or a traffic signal. Wherever you are, whatever it is, it is good—potentially at least. You will find that "there is but one Presence and one Power in the universe, the Good omnipotent." All its gifts can be good. Give thanks and you'll come to believe in this.

When you pray, give thanks in advance for that for which you ask, as though already received. It works miracles.

Giving thanks, the grateful attitude, does affect the attitude of all the people who serve you or help you or can help you. People respond to thanks, to praise, which is about the same thing. Sometimes it is like a blood transfusion. You may not always see what it does, but it quickens people's lives; often it saves them. You have only to watch patiently for the effect to see it work. It transforms people's relations to you. But it transforms your relations to everything. It transforms everything for you. Why? Because it transforms you. It transforms your thinking, and your thinking creates your circumstances.

Sometimes I think we need no other formula for triumphant living but this simple rule, this one-word recipe, thanksgiving. For gratitude is simply awareness, consciousness intensified, of good; and consciousness of good is what brings it into manifestation. Nationally, officially, we give one day a year to thanksgiving. In our churches, we give one day a week perhaps. But personally one minute a minute is a duty, an opportunity, a privilege. How much is enough? Well how much air is enough, how much cleanliness, how much security?

The thankful attitude wins out. It frees us from fear; it creates good will; it builds harmony; it secures peace. It plants perfect seed; it is crop insurance. It promotes health. A by-product of it is unfailing, unquailing courage. It builds faith that removes mountains. It answers prayers. It brings conscious well-being and unconscious strength. It fires ambition and enthusiasm; it clears the vision. It releases innate powers and increases skills. It guides and inspires. It produces energy and spurs initiative. It takes God into partnership. It pleases God, not because it flatters Him—oh, no!—but because it complies with His law. It makes happiness, for others and for you.

Make a list of your heart's desires. Scan it. Take it item by item and begin giving thanks for the portion of each you have. You will find you have much more than you think and you will find it all increasing as your thankfulness grows. You will soon find that trying to enumerate the blessings that come of the thankful attitude is like attempting to count the rays of sunlight that flood your world when you open your life to the sun. For thanksgiving is a key to the door of consciousness that leads to knowledge of God.

How shall you practice thanksgiving? Practice it deliberately, all the time, where you are, everywhere. Here is how David the Psalmist did it:

"Bless Jehovah, O my soul;
And all that is within me, *bless* his holy name.
Bless Jehovah, O my soul,
And forget not all his benefits:
Who forgiveth all thine iniquities;
Who healeth all thy diseases;
Who redeemeth thy life from destruction;
Who crowneth thee with lovingkindness and tender
     mercies;
Who satisfieth thy desire with good things,
So that thy youth is renewed . . ."

This is the crowning form of thanksgiving that includes all thanksgiving. Can we carry this praise-prayer in our heart without the thankful attitude and refrain from thank-you's to everybody everywhere along our way.

We can serve God only through our service to His creatures, and thanks to them is thanks to Him. It is doing His work and spreading His good. And "thereby good shall come unto thee."

A Formula for Prosperity

JOHN D. MURPHY

VARIOUS SCHEMES have been worked out for getting rich quick. Most of them fail, but there is one formula that has never yet failed to enrich the person who used it. It is as certain in its operation as the law of gravitation because it is based upon principles that are as sure and unfailing as any physical law. It is God's own prosperity plan and it has proved itself in actual practice many times.

Take the case of Kenneth S. Keyes as an example. Keyes decided to go to Florida to get in on the boom. The boom burst just about the time he arrived in Miami, and he found himself in bad shape financially. But after a while he happened upon this prosperity formula. The first year he used it his income increased sixty per cent. The next year his income jumped one hundred per cent. It increased until the Keyes company became the largest real-estate company in the State of Florida and in one year grossed over thirteen million dollars.

Mr. Keyes taught the formula to one of his salesmen who found himself in debt. Within one year the salesman had paid off his indebtedness and had a sizable bank account. He became so successful that he went into business for himself and was soon making more than fifteen thousand dollars a year.

Or consider the case of R. G. LeTourneau. In early middle age, he found himself heavily in debt. He had a family to support and only a grammar-school education. His case looked hopeless. But he too discovered this formula and put it to work. He became the head of the company that is the world's largest maker of earth-moving machinery and does well over forty million dollars worth of business annually. He has established schools for under-privileged children. He has founded the world's largest charitable organization, the LeTourneau Foundation.

William Colgate started using this formula when, a poor boy, he went out into the world to seek his fortune. He founded one of the largest soap businesses in the world. Heinz pickles are known all over the world, but it is not generally known that Heinz used this formula to build his success. Kraft cheese is a household word today. Mr. Kraft also learned about the formula in his early business career. The list of successful men who have used it would be too long to print here.

One of the most amazing things about the formula is that more people do not use it. For it is no closely guarded secret. You yourself have heard of it many times. But perhaps it seems too simple. Perhaps you can see no reason why it should work. Perhaps you have never analyzed the principles that make the formula work. The purpose of this article is not to introduce you to some new secret but to induce you to try an old one.

The formula is simple. It consists in taking God into partnership and agreeing to give Him ten per cent of the proceeds of your business. Ten per cent isn't much to give a partner who is all-wise and all-powerful.

The divine principles under which this formula operates are not unusual or mysterious but can be observed functioning throughout nature. They are:

(1) There is one basic substance, whose source is God. This one substance is manifested in various forms such as energy, health, prosperity, sustenance, and the like. Money is only a symbol of one of the forms of this one substance.

(2) This basic substance, regardless of the form it may take, must flow through some channel or be provided with an outlet as well as an inlet.

(3) Before this substance can be available a channel must be prepared for it.

(4) There is a basic unity underlying all creation, which inseparably unites the good of the individual with the good of the whole.

In considering the "flow through," think for a moment of a large water wheel with millions of tons of water backed up behind it. The inlet is open. But the outlet is closed so that the water cannot flow. As long as this condition exists the wheel can realize no power. Or consider what happens when you turn on an electric switch. The electricity is there in the wire all the time, but when the switch is off the current is stopped from flowing. When you throw the switch you close the circuit so the electrical power can flow through. Before our lungs can be filled with air they must be emptied, and to realize the power of the divine substance we must open our inlet and our outlet gates and allow it to flow through us.

Jesus understood this law when He instructed us "Give, and it shall be given unto you" and stated "it is more blessed to give than to receive." The influx of divine ideas, which is the basis of all prosperity, obeys this law. Shortly after LeTourneau started tithing he received an idea, apparently out of the thin air, concerning a new type of road machine. This idea started him on his road to fortune, and since that time he has continued to receive the kind of ideas he needed when he needed them. One of his engineers told me, "We don't know where he gets all those ideas of his, but most of them are not only good but new and revolutionary."

Before we can receive divine substance we must prepare a receptacle for it.

The receptacle for divine substance, in whatever form, is always a need for that substance which has been created in accordance with its legitimate use. Consider, for example, how this works out in the case of the polar bear, whose white coat is provided automatically simply because he needs it.

Tithing creates this legitimate need for more

prosperity; the prosperity flows to us automatically. Spending money recklessly or foolishly will not have this same result. This does not create a legitimate need; rather it is apt to leave us needy. Just as we would not give a child ten dollars to spend on lollipops, God will not increase our supply merely because we spend our money foolishly on ourselves. Legitimate use is a condition that Jesus stressed. Using a portion of our income to further the spiritual evolution of man or to help our brother in some other way is righteousness.

There is no sin in being rich. To be rich is sinful only when riches are not used properly. Until it is used wealth does no one any good, not even the man who owns it. In Jesus' parable of the talents the servants who used their talents were rewarded with more; but the servant who buried his talent in the ground had even that one talent taken from him.

There is a basic unity that makes the good of the individual the good of the whole.

There is one great inclusive whole in which all individuals are parts, just as the individual cells of the human body join together to make one man. Jesus used the phrase "Thou art made whole" in curing disease. The same principles that are used in healing the body work in healing lack of prosperity. Since we are all but "members" of the one body, as Paul expressed it, we cannot help others without helping ourselves. When the hand pulls a thorn from the foot the hand is also helping itself, for it is helping the body upon which both the hand and the foot are dependent for their existence. Jesus illustrated this unity by the statement "I am the true vine, ye are the branches," And when each man ceases to regard himself as a separate, individual entity entirely apart from mankind and comes to see himself as but one of the "branches" or members which make up the body of humanity, he cannot fail to see that whatever he does to help others helps him and whatever he does to hurt others inevitably hurts him.

When we tithe, we are helping other members of the great body of mankind of which we are also a part. This being true, it is literally impossible for us not to realize beneficial results.

This formula worked for Henry P. Crowell of Quaker Oats; M. W. Baldwin, the railway equipment manufacturer; and many other successful men. In a few years after he began tithing Mr. Keyes found that the tenth he gave to God was more than his entire income had ever been before. William Colgate's business prospered so much from tithing that soon he was giving more than a tenth. He kept increasing the amount until finally he was giving half his income and still he was prospered. At last he gave his entire income.

This formula is waiting for you to use it. A good agent or broker would charge you much more than ten per cent to obtain additional business

for you. He could never give you the "breaks,"
"hunches," new ideas, and all sorts of good things
that your unseen Partner can bring you. God Himself has guaranteed the formula: "Prove me now
herewith, saith Jehovah of hosts, if I will not open
you the windows of heaven, and pour you out a
blessing, that there shall not be room enough *to
receive it."*

You Are What You Think

ELLSWORTH KALAS

WHEN Victor Lindlahr published a book in 1940, entitled "You Are What You Eat," it caught the fancy of the nation and within six months was enjoying its third printing. The title became something of a byword in this nation, which is so quick to snatch up catch phrases, until thousands of Americans became very conscious of the importance of their diet to their healthy enjoyment of everyday life.

More recently medical science has begun emphasizing another study, which has been aptly termed "psychosomatic medicine." With apologies to Mr. Lindlahr, I like to state the practical factors of psychosomatic medicine this way: You are what you think.

This, of course, is an old, old truth to the followers of Jesus. We have long realized that "as he [man] thinketh within himself, so is he." We know from experience and observation that if a man continually thinks meanness he becomes the very personification of meanness; while the person who fills his mind with thoughts of peace and kindness gains a serenity that is beautiful.

Now science comes to substantiate the teachings

of the Book with reams of case histories, clinical tests, and authoritative opinions. Some of the statements of medical men concerning the relationship of the thought life to physical and mental health are so startling that even those of us who have always believed are taken aback.

Hippocrates, the father of medicine, hinted of the relationship centuries ago when he suggested that anger and fear breed a poison in the blood. Now it has been clinically demonstrated that the amount of poison released into the blood stream of a person by a fit of anger is sometimes powerful enough to kill insects or small animals!

What does this poison do to the human body? Well, an outburst of anger frequently sends a person's blood pressure spiraling as much as sixty points higher. It is easy to see what that can do to a person suffering from a weak heart. John Hunter, the famous Scottish surgeon, often said that his life was in the hands of any man who chose to annoy him; yet knowing this, Hunter allowed himself to become unduly irritated one day and suffered a fatal attack during a fit of temper.

But it is not only a violent temper that can break a man. Dr. Flanders Dunbar, of Columbia University's College of Physicians and Surgeons, has declared that an upset mind can bring on heart disease, stomach ulcers, asthma, tuberculosis, or diabetes, and that if a person is already afflicted with one of these ailments the condition will be aggravated severely by unhealthy thoughts. A Scotch authority on rheumatic diseases has estimated that no less than forty per cent of rheumatic cases are psychological in origin. Dr. Dunbar believes further that eighty per cent of all accidents spring from a neurotic basis.

All of us can recall everyday examples that demonstrate the physical effect of thought. There is the anxious housewife who works all day to prepare for the evening's guests—and by the time the guests arrive is suffering from headache and nervous nausea. More than one high-school or college teacher has smiled facetiously at the extraordinary absenteeism on the day of a stiff examination; yet it is true enough that many students suffer colds, fever, and headaches simply from fearful anticipation of what the examination may hold for them. I can still remember (and if I should ever forget, the grade records of a large university can remind me) the day I took a final examination in German and found myself so troubled by a throbbing headache that my mind refused to function efficiently. It was the first and only headache I ever suffered. William Gladstone, one of England's greatest prime ministers, always contracted a cold the night before a crucial or dreaded debate. Sir William Osler advised his coleagues in the medical profession that the future of tuberculars depended more on what they had in their heads than on what was in their chests.

How sensitively organized is this human body!

A man driving home from work allows the conduct of another motorist to irritate him. Instead of overcoming this evil thought with good, he allows it to boil in his mind. As a result, the lovely meal prepared by his wife brings him indigestion and the poor lady of the house wonders what she did wrong. The evil thoughts breed and multiply, and by the time our friend retires for the night he has found half a dozen more reasons to be irritated. These evils prey on his mind and drive sleep from him. When finally he does fall asleep, his rest is fitful, and he awakens in the morning more than ready to bite off a dozen heads before noon.

All of this sounds pretty negative. But it is encouraging to remember that good thoughts are as capable of bringing health and success as bad thoughts are of destroying. Paul summed up the secret of happy living so beautifully and practically that none of us needs to live any other way. He recommended: "Finally, brethren, whatsoever things are true, whatsoever things are honorable, whatsoever things are just, whatsoever things are pure, whatsoever things are lovely, whatsoever things are of good report; if there be any virtue, and if there be any praise, think on these things."

It is generally agreed that Paul wrote these words while he was confined in a Roman prison, chained to a Roman soldier. He wrote from experience. If he had allowed himself in those circumstances to think about things around him, he would have been engulfed by fear and doubt. Instead he thought about true, honest, just, and lovely things so that he could continue a few lines later, "I have learned, in whatsoever state I am, therein to be content."

A friend complained to me not long ago that a business associate was undermining him. "And," he concluded, "I don't want any milk-and-honey platitudes now about 'loving him.' I want something practical."

"If it's something practical you want," I replied, "there's nothing better for me to say than: 'Keep loving him.' More than that, let me urge you to think the most uplifting and pure thoughts you can possibly manage. If the man is undermining you, as you believe, you need to be alert and to think clearly. What he can do to your reputation is not half so dangerous as what he can do inside of you if you allow bitterness and anger to corrode your mind. Already this situation has troubled you until you are losing sleep. I'll venture to say that the efficiency of your work is breaking down. Try the advice of Jesus and pray for the man. Whatever it may mean to him, I guarantee it will mean pure thoughts and happiness for you."

It was less than a week later that my friend returned, smiling radiantly. "It worked!" he said. "I prayed for Len, and my own attitude changed. Since then we've resolved our difficulties and we're getting along beautifully."

It is surprising to see how very easy it is to follow Paul's admonition to "think on these things."
Think of the simple experiences in everyday living,
the little situations that are so ordinary and sometimes trip us more emphatically than the crucial
matters do. Perhaps I pass an old friend on the
street, and he fails to respond to my cheery hello. It
is possible in such a case to think about the supposed
slight until I am thoroughly bitter inside. Instead
I'll obey Paul and think about a lovely thing: "That
man has been one of my truest friends for years; he
has stood by me through thick and thin." And miraculously my thoughts are serene and stimulating. I
go on about the day's activities with the vigor of a
healthy mind.

Fortunately there are many just, pure, and lovely
things about which we can think. The beauty of the
sky, of a bird in flight, of a delicate flower in
bloom—all of these inspire pure thoughts that
serve to purge the mind. The recalling of past
blessings, of answered prayers—these too turn our
thinking into healthy channels. Best of all, we can
always remember the words of the Bible, the promises of reward for faith, the encouragement to believe. Such thoughts will flood our life with every
kind of blessing.

Perhaps it is well to mention that, since we are
what we think, it is good to watch our diet—our
mental diet, that is. We can make it much easier
for ourself by feeding our mind the right fare in the

first place. What I read, the conversations I listen to, the radio programs that enter my home, all are an influence on my thinking. If I insist on burdening my mind with the sordid and unpleasant I shall find it very hard to "think on these things." But if in my reading and listening I choose to feed my mind well, I have come a long way toward victorious thinking and living.

In its study of psychosomatic medicine, science has pointed up for us the dangers of the wrong kind of thoughts. God will show us, in the experiences of our daily life, the blessings that come when we think right. And no matter how elementary the statement may seem, it is an inviolable law: We are what we think. If we choose to think of the evil and to feed our mind on what is base and unclean, our life will gradually become the embodiment of these qualities. But if we earnestly strive to think on the good, the beautiful, the pure, we shall find ourselves attaining these qualities. And we shall find too that good thoughts are fertile; that they bring forth more of their kind, until good has so filled our mind that there is no room for the evil and unkind.

God will help us in our efforts to think right. We may pray in faith for Him to fill our mind with thoughts that are pleasing to Him and consistent with the spirit of Jesus Christ. And as we put the thought-law to work for us, we learn the blessings that await those who "think on these things."

Miracles without Mystery

CLINTON E. BERNARD

A BUSINESSMAN answers his desk telephone. A voice says to him: "This is Jim. I'm feeling low. Are you too busy to talk with me awhile if I come in?" The businessman scarcely glances at the work piled high on his desk. Without a trace of reluctance in his voice he answers: "Of course I'm not too busy. Come on over. I'll see you right away." He will not slight such a call; he dare not, for he belongs to an army of minutemen who can remain secure only if they help others to remain secure. He is an "A.A."; more formally he is a member—as is Jim—of the group called Alcoholics Anonymous.

Our businessman knows from bitter experience that Jim is feeling low because he wants a drink of liquor—many drinks, copious drinks. As a fellow A.A. he must help to dissipate the craving.

What does he talk about when the slipping A.A. comes into the office? Probably he says nothing that the casual hearer would think sublime or even significant. He does not preach. The conversation may run something like this:

"Jim, how did you feel when you woke up this morning?"

"Fine," Jim answers.

"And do you remember how you used to feel when you woke up after a bender? You felt as if your nerves were red hot, and your thoughts were hammering on them. Or maybe you felt like a lot of devils were inside you and trying to claw their way out. Remember?"

"Sure I remember," Jim growls. "Ought to."

"And you wondered, as well as a man in your condition could wonder about anything sensible, what disgraceful things you had done during the time when liquor was in charge of your mind. Did your wife know? Did your boss know—or did you have a boss? Would you ever be able to hold up your head and act like a man again?

"Now contrast that with the way you woke up this morning. You felt fine. Your wife was pleasant; your children thought their old man was a pretty good skate after all. You didn't have a furtive feeling when you met a policeman. You had a job. You could go to the job and look the boss in the eye, knowing you were a valuable employee and he wanted to keep you.

"You know how all this miracle of improvement came about. You couldn't whip liquor but you got the help of a power that was stronger than liquor— that is stronger than liquor. You have a group of friends who are always ready to help you when you feel yourself slipping. You're too smart——"

"That's enough," Jim interrupts. He is grinning. "I'm all right now. Thanks."

"Don't thank me," the other replies. "I got more out of it than you did." And he is telling the truth—as Jim knows.

Alcoholics Anonymous cannot be called an organization for it has no central executive group, no officers, no bylaws or constitution, no dues. An alcoholic begins living by its principles and is placed on the safe path of sobriety. The way of life he has adopted is a very practical one: to remain safe he must help save others. Frequently a member moves to a new home in another city. There he becomes the nucleus of a new A.A. group. But he may not proselyte the unwilling no matter how desperately they need his message. He may help only where his services are welcomed.

Fundamentally of course the work grows because it is sound, because it really does save men and women from a scourge that physicians and psychiatrists have been helpless to heal.

The program is outlined in twelve steps as set forth by Alcoholics Anonymous. The twelve steps are stated thus:

"1. We admitted we were powerless over alcohol—that our lives had become unmanageable.

"2. Came to believe that a Power greater than ourselves could restore us to sanity.

"3. Made a decision to turn our will and our lives over to the care of God as we understood Him.

"4. Made a searching and fearless moral inventory of ourselves.

"5. Admitted to God, to ourselves, and to another human being the exact nature of our wrongs.

"6. Were entirely ready to have God remove all these defects of character.

"7. Humbly asked Him to remove our shortcomings.

"8. Made a list of all persons we had harmed and became willing to make amends to them all.

"9. Made direct amends to such people wherever possible, except when to do so would injure them or others.

"10. Continued to take personal inventory and when we were wrong promptly admitted it.

"11. Sought through prayer and meditation to improve our conscious contact with God as we understood Him, praying only for knowledge of His will for us and the power to carry that out.

"12. Having had a spiritual experience as the result of these steps, we tried to carry this message to alcoholics and to practice these principles in all our affairs."

This looks like a religious program. The A.A. members call it a program of spiritual principles. Although many of them are church members, in presenting this program they studiously avoid anything resembling religious cant or sectarianism. They assert that they deal with spiritual principles that are common to all religious denominations. Note that when they speak of God in their twelve-step program they say, "God as we understood Him."

They sell their idea successfully to those of all denominations—and to those of no denomination. To the agnostic they say:

"Let us make haste to reassure you. We found that as soon as we were able to lay aside prejudice and express even a willingness to believe in a power greater than ourselves we commenced to get results, even though it was impossible for any of us to define fully or comprehend that power, which is God.

"Much to our relief, we discovered we did not need to consider another's conception of God. Our own conception, however inadequate, was sufficient to make the approach and to effect a contact with Him. As soon as we admitted the possible existence of a creative intellect, a Spirit of the universe underlying the totality of things, we began to be possessed of a new sense of power and direction, provided we took other simple steps. We found that God does not make too hard terms with those who seek Him."

There is an old theory that heaven keeps books; that if a person wants help from God he had better improve his credit standing with heaven by helping somebody else first. The A.A. believes in this theory. If he does not believe in it at first, circumstance soon convinces him. He must try to help other alcoholics to sobriety; if he neglects doing so he will begin drinking again. The literature of Alcoholics Anonymous states this positively; experience confirms it. Literally the A.A. can be sure of safety from liquor only if he leads a good life, if he does what all good Christians are supposed to do. He is sand-bagged into goodness, but he soon learns not to mind this for he has found the answer to his most pressing problem.

"There is a solution" is the flat assertion made by the book called "Alcoholics Anonymous," which might well be called the textbook of the A.A. fraternity. "The great fact is just this, and nothing less: that we have had deep and effective spiritual experiences, which have revolutionized our whole attitude toward life, toward our fellows, and toward God's universe. The central fact of our lives today is the absolute certainty that our Creator has entered into our hearts and lives in a way which is indeed miraculous. He has commenced to accomplish those things for us which we could never do for ourselves."

A.A.'s have considerable social life in their own group. The writer of this article was permitted to attend one of the weekly meetings of a group, where about sixty persons were gathered for a short business meeting and a social good time and refreshments (coffee and food). There was nothing unusual looking about the people in the group except that they appeared to be above the average. (And the A.A. members come from all strata of society.) The speakers (who were limited to five minutes each) spoke with conviction. One of them, a successful salesman, was orator enough to charm almost any audience. The casual visitor was struck with the light attitude of the A.A.'s toward their past. Liquor had whipped them; they admitted it cheerfully—for they had substituted divine will for human will and so were secure.

There was one neophyte, a pale young woman, who was attending her first A.A. meeting. She sat in on one of the "jam sessions" that followed the meeting. Presently her reserve was thawed by the atmosphere of frankness prevalent there, and she talked.

"I've been an alcoholic since I was fourteen," she said. "My longest dry stretch was six months. Liquor has cost me four jobs in the last three weeks. I don't think I ever would get so I could handle the stuff."

"That's right," agreed an A.A. pleasantly. "It's rank poison to you. You're an alcoholic."

"I'll say I am," the girl agreed. A muscle in her cheek twitched.

"But," the older A.A. went on, "the fact that you can't handle liquor needn't harm you or make your life unhappy. Some people are allergic to pollen and get hay fever from it. I've an aunt who breaks out with something like hives every time she eats strawberries—so she doesn't eat them. You're allergic to liquor. You can't take it, not even a little of it, but you can learn to leave it alone. And if you get into our principles, learn what is really behind them, and live by them, you've got more than a cure for alcoholism; you've got a design for happy living."

"But do you ever lose the craving?" asked the pale girl. Her cheek muscle twitched again. "It wouldn't be any fun to have to struggle with it all the time."

"You don't have to face an eternity of wanting a drink," the salesman reassured her. "Even now you don't want to stay drunk all the time, do you?"

"Sometimes I don't think much about it for weeks," the girl stated. "But when it does come——"

"There you are," the salesman interrupted (and only the best of salesmen know exactly when to interrupt). "You have to live only one day at a time. In the morning when you wake up, ask God—your idea of God—to keep you safe from liquor for that one day and depend on Him to do it. You can't live more than one day at a time, so there's no use in being anxious about tomorrow or next year. Keep asking God to help you. In a pinch ask your A.A. friends to help you too. They'll do it no matter what else they have been doing. They won't dare refuse you—and they won't want to. The periods of wanting a drink will grow farther and farther apart until finally you will find you have lost active desire."

"Oh, it's like that," the pale girl commented.

The salesman looked at her intently. "Maybe," he surmised, "you expect a miracle to happen to you right away. It can happen, but in the majority of cases it doesn't.

"I remember I was expecting that same miracle and was disappointed when it did not appear. I was getting along all right—hadn't had a drink in over six months—but I still wanted my miracle.

"One evening I was making a business trip by car. I grew thirsty and stopped at a roadhouse for an orangeade. The place was serving hard liquor too. I was the only man at the bar with a soft drink. The place reeked with liquor. I drank my orangeade and went on. Then I realized that I had had my miracle.

"I had gone into a bar where everybody else was drinking hard stuff. I had ordered a soft drink and drunk it and gone on about my business without even thinking about wanting a drink of hard liquor myself! Yes, there was my miracle."

He smiled pleasantly and walked away—good salesman that he was. Soon he was shouting with laughter with a group on the other side of the room. And this brings to mind another A.A. principle.

"We have been dealing with alcohol in its worst aspects," they say, "but we aren't a glum lot. If newcomers could see no joy or fun in our existence they wouldn't want it. We absolutely insist on enjoying life."

They do enjoy life, these people of A.A. The full spirit of conviviality that once contributed to their downfall now helps to keep them upright. The salesman grasps his coffee cup and strides over to the coffee table.

"Another shot of Java," he orders. "But it's got to be a hundred proof. And no chaser."

The woman who presides at the coffee urn smiles in understanding. The jest, as she knows, is more than a jest. It is a declaration of independence uttered by one who is so confident of his freedom that he can speak lightly of the time when he was in slavery. The world talks of war, but what of that? He depends on God for help—and God never goes to war.

(Alcoholics Anonymous may be contacted by writing P. O. Box 658, Church Street Annex, New York City.)

The Source of Security

GARDNER HUNTING

"SOME People Have All the Accidents" was the title of an article published recently, an article written by a man who has made a specialty of studying accident records. He said, "Some people appear to be accident-prone; they continually meet with disaster."

He arrayed a long list of case histories that seemed to show that fate singles out certain individuals as special victims of misfortune, pursuing them as if it were the hound of calamity forever on the trail of these helpless hares. He included people whose daily lives seem to be fraught with "happenings" that, through no fault of their own, bring painful results upon them; people who are always cutting their fingers, falling down stairs, slipping in the bathtub, catching the new epidemic, colliding with other people's cars; people who seem to be victims of what is commonly called bad luck.

Taking all the appearances in their cases at face value you might easily conclude that the title of his article was justified; that some people really are always unlucky and the "breaks" always do go against them; that chances are always mischances for them; that they are doomed to crashes, crack-ups,

152

and other forms of misfortune. But, being a scientist, he believed in cause and effect, and his purpose was not to collect a mass of terrifying facts but to search out the causes of such effects. His conclusion was interesting.

Looking beneath and beyond appearances, he discovered that people who seem to be accident-prone are people who are prone to "emotional disturbances"; that is, people who are always worried about something, people who are habitually afraid, people who carry burdens of anxiety, anger, animosity, antipathy—anything that sets up strife or struggle or dread. In fact the final finding of his survey was that it is fear that makes men and women, you and me, Tom, Dick, and Harriet, subject to accident.

Now you and I could easily array a lot of case histories that would match those this writer assembled. We know people who seem to be continually out of luck. But let's take a leaf out of this scientist's book and look, not at the accident record that scares us but beneath and beyond at great realities, not searching even for causes but for cures.

In the 91st Psalm is the promise:

"There shall no evil befall thee,

Neither shall any plague come nigh thy tent."

And this promise is made to those who "abide under the shadow of the Almighty."

If we spend our time studying the accident records, dwelling on appearances, taking so-called facts at face value, we shall become emotionally disturbed.

If we "have faith in God," as Jesus said; if we "love one another," as His commandment instructed us; if we do to others as we would that they should do to us, we shall find out that the Psalmist and Jesus meant what they said, and that what they said was true when they said it and is true now.

Faith in God will cure emotional disturbance; perfect love will cast out fear. Taking Jesus at His word will prevent you and me from being accident-prone.

"He will give his angels charge over thee,
To keep thee in all thy ways."

If? If what? If we stop trying to live without Him, and just tie up to faith in His goodness and love and fatherliness and faithfulness; if we let go of fear and self-management and self-seeking and all kinds of selfishness, and dwell "in the secret place of the Most High," which is the kingdom of love and peace.

Is it harder to nurse faith in the good than to cherish fear? The hardest thing in life is to live with fear. It causes emotional disturbances. It is the cause of accident—ranging all the way from stumbling on the stairs to fumbling in closing a sale. Fear of my boss, fear of my rival, fear of my customer, fear of debt, fear of treachery, fear of my own stupidity, fear of circumstances—fear, fear, fear is my worst enemy. Fear of interruption, of disappointment, of failure, of man or woman or circumstance—that is what we stumble and fumble over.

It seems hard to believe that just letting go of fear and taking hold of faith will heal all diseases and redeem our life from destruction—but it will. Just letting go of the impulse to struggle and hurry and fight for our own and taking hold of the purpose simply to become channels for God's goodness to others will cure our own troubles, solve our own difficulties, fulfill our heart's desires, make our career successful, our business prosperous, our life happy. It will.

Jesus said, "Fear not, only believe." Believe what? Believe in "the way, and the truth, and the life" that He taught and lived. Our commonest trouble in accepting His way of life with faith is that we are in a hurry to get results. Well, one of the most helpful things we can do is to forget about results. The farmer's job is to plant good seed and see that it is properly cultivated. Our concern is to plant good seed thoughts and to cultivate them. Then we can let God manage the results.

Are you afraid of something? Face it with the purpose to plant good seed of "good will toward men" and your fear will vanish like your breath from a windowpane. Your vision will clear, your purpose become definite, your thinking become lucid. Your skill will be released; your wits will work with ease and precision; your courage will fill you with power as breathing fills your lungs with air. Good will (love) will give you inspiration on any and all occasions—when you are "called on the carpet," when you meet sales resistance, when you encounter criticism, hostility, treachery, accident.

If you will just follow this one rule, tie up to this one principle, "appearances" of mishap and misfortune will disappear from your life, and you will find that any survey you make of your experience will lead you to one sure conclusion:

There is no such thing as an accident. Every effect has a cause, and the cause of security is faith in God.

Faith will not only remove mountains, it will also remove failure and frustration and fear. It will remove trouble and grief and despair. It will remove sorrow and wretchedness and misery. "Your Father knoweth what things ye have need of."

If you think you haven't faith enough, just take this to heart: Faith enough to start living by the idea that God is good and that He is the one and only presence and power in the universe is faith enough. "Seek ye first his kingdom, and his righteousness; and all these things shall be added unto you." *Seek* —that is what you have to do. Just seek and keep on seeking. Let go of fear, of emotional disturbances due to fear, and security will be added to you—yes, and success and achievement and supply and friends and usefulness. And "it is not yet made manifest what shall be," for "Eye hath not seen, nor ear heard, neither have entered into the heart of man the things which God hath prepared for them that love him." What success, what achievement, what security, what prize can possibly compare with this?

"But," you say, "I can't control what 'happens' to me simply by believing that nothing bad can happen." Quite so—but if you can swim, falling into the water won't hurt you, will it? If you have faith that the water will support you, you won't sink. And swimming—what is swimming? Fun, isn't it, when you are not afraid?

Perhaps you say, "But suppose my circumstances are hopeless; suppose I have an incurable affliction; suppose I am surrounded by insuperable difficulties."

Well, my friend, did Jesus ever recognize any difficulty as insuperable, any afflicted one as incurable? He did not. He said, "According to your faith be it done unto you." He proved it in His own life, didn't He, in His own overcoming, in His healing, in His resurrection?

The promises are made to us on condition that we follow instructions, keep the commandments. "Have faith in God," "Love one another," "All things therefore whatsoever ye would that men should do unto you, even so do ye also unto them," "Give," "Love," "Trust," "Cast thy burden upon Jehovah," "Be not anxious," "Judge not," "Come unto me," "Seek ye first his kingdom," "Abide under the shadow of the Almighty." If you will do these things "there shall no evil befall thee."

Just Listen

RUSSELL W. LAKE

WHEN we were children we read about big genii that popped up out of nowhere in response to someone's rubbing a certain magic lamp. The genii fulfilled every request, performed extraordinary feats. It seemed that nothing was too much to ask of them. With wide-eyed amazement we read about all those wonderful things that happened. Young as we were, we knew they couldn't really be true, but it was very nice to think about them anyway.

A great many years had to pass before we finally came to the realization that there is, after all, a little genie—our own private genie. Of course he isn't a little elf with a brown stocking cap and extended shoes with the tips turned up. Nor is he a giant who appears in a cloud of smoke when we rub a little copper lamp of very strange design. He doesn't bow low before us and say: "What is your will, Master? Ask, and it shall be done."

It isn't quite so simple as that. But our own genie is as powerful as the ones of which we used to read —even more powerful. We don't have to rub the lamp to bring him; he is always here, protecting us, advising, pointing out the right way. If you want to know what is the right thing to do in any circumstance, just ask him. And then listen. He never fails to answer and he is invariably right.

When we get older we don't call him our genie any more. We call him God.

Well, if we have a voice within us that keeps telling us what is right for us to do, then why do we do such crazy things sometimes? Reach over and turn on your radio and then move the knob back and forth across a station setting. You'll see what I mean. You have to concentrate on it and get the correct tuning before the message comes in clear.

I have done many amazingly stupid things in my life, and they weren't done because of the voice within me but in spite of it. I didn't listen; I had a louder station tuned in that drowned it out. And yet I believe that by and large I have heard the voice and followed its direction without knowing I was doing so. There is a pattern in everyone's life, and while sometimes it may seem more like a jigsaw puzzle, all the parts somehow will fit into place.

When I was quite young I had the idea that I would like to be a writer of fiction. Writers, I thought, always lived in sumptuous palaces; people hung on their every word; they worked when they felt like it; and loafed when they didn't want to work. So I sat down and pounded out some stories. I sent them to editors and eagerly waited for the checks. With monotonous regularity the stories came back—minus checks.

I was more than crestfallen—I was desolate. But now in my older wisdom I am glad I didn't sell those stories. I was not ready to write. I was not mature. I didn't go about it in the right way. I did not even want to write; I just wanted to be a writer. If I had sold those awful stories, it would have been a very bad thing for me. In that instance my life was directed away from harm without my knowing it and certainly without my appreciating it.

In the years that followed I went my way, just blundering ahead. Sometimes it seemed my life had no particular point, but in retrospect it all makes a recognizable pattern.

For almost twenty years, I have been a salesman in varied lines of business and in different types of selling. In twenty years of close application one should learn something about a subject. Last year I suddenly conceived the idea that I ought to use my experience to help others iron out some of their problems. I don't remember what I was doing when the idea first came to me. I don't even remember in what form it came or what specific occurrence caused it to crystallize. That's the way with those things. The first thing you know there the idea is, all formed and shaped.

At any rate, I was pushed—actually pushed from within—to write an article. I wrote it and sent it to Sales Management. It sold immediately. I wrote others. They sold. I wrote articles and sent them to Printers' Ink, and they were accepted. I wrote articles and sent them to Advertising and Selling. They too were accepted. Now what do you think of that?

I'm not finished—certainly not. I'm going on and on because I've got a voice within me that is telling me what to do. And I'm listening.

If you are like I am you have to be careful to be sure you are hearing the right voice. I've always been an impulsive person and I've battered my head against so many walls that I have come to regard a new idea with something akin to suspicion. But I find now that I needn't worry. If I give the idea careful scrutiny from all angles and enough thought and time to allow it either to die or to flourish, I can't go wrong. If the idea is right and you give it proper treatment, it will force itself upon you.

It is a comforting thought that each of us has within himself all knowledge, all wisdom, all good. It is there clamoring to manifest itself in our life, beseeching us to listen and, having heard, to act. There is a divine pattern in my life, as there is in yours. Perhaps you and I don't yet know quite what it is. Maybe we are not sure just where our steps are leading us, but if we have listened closely and are doing what we are being told to do we can be sure we are on the right highway to fulfill our divine destiny.

The highway takes strange turns sometimes. A young friend of mine was a bookkeeper in an office, but he always had wanted to be a salesman. His company went bankrupt, and he was out of a job.

Domestic responsibilities made it imperative that he maintain an income, but at the time there were no bookkeeping jobs to be had. Almost immediately he fell into an opportunity to become an electrician, which was a far cry from either bookkeeping or salesmanship. The job was handed to him, practically forced on him. He went in as an apprentice and he worked hard and studied. He studied while he was working and he studied books at night and week ends. Later he went to night school. The idea of selling still was in the back of his head, but at that time it did not plague him and make him miserable. He was satisfied with his job and very much interested in electricity.

A few years later an opportunity presented itself, and he became a sales engineer for an electrical equipment manufacturer. That's the way his pattern worked itself out.

The voice within me is telling me to do thus and so. At least, I think it is. When I am sure, I shall not hesitate. In such a case it doesn't take any courage to act, because I know in advance I can't go wrong. God within me is striving to make my life fuller, happier, more successful. My part is to co-operate and allow Him to do it.

Listen to that voice. If you hear no answer to your question it is your fault, not God's. You can't listen with the radio blaring in your ear or with your mind full of resentment or hate or worry. Work definitely to let yourself go, to recapture the faith of a child. There is nothing to worry about anyway. Retire within yourself, place your problems and your desires before God—and then listen. You will not be telling God anything He does not already know, but it gives Him a better chance to talk to you when your mind is consciously attuned to Him.

Your method of conversing with God may be different from mine, but it doesn't matter so long as we achieve the same results. Each morning when I arise and each night before I go to bed, I go where I can be alone and quiet and free of outer distractions. I relax in a chair and close my eyes and thank God for the blessings He has given me and for His blessings that are still to come. I acknowledge that God is all-good, all-power, and that all the good that comes into my life comes from Him. I ask Him to guide me, to point out the way He would have me go. If I have a particular problem I lay it before Him and ask Him for guidance. Many times during the day when circumstances arise requiring decisions I turn to God and say: "What shall I do?"

I do not prostrate myself or grovel or beg. He is my Father, a kind and wise Father, who is lavish in giving me all that is good for me to have. I know that He wants me to have happiness, success, prosperity, and He will provide these things if only I will do my part in accepting them. So I ask him what course I should take in order that His will may work through me. And then I listen.

Sometimes the full answer does not develop at

once. Sometimes it suddenly comes to me later in the day or during the night or even a few days later. But it always comes. I have been consistently rewarded for following these instructions.

Just as there is great reward for following the guidance of the inner voice, there is a corresponding penalty for ignoring it. The penalty is not of God's doing. It is just that when you try to impose your human will contrary to God's will you come to grief because you are bound to be wrong. The penalty you bring on yourself manifests itself in varying degrees of failure, unhappiness, poverty.

The divine plan of your life and my life is success, happiness, prosperity. Jesus promised us that. The plan is laid out for us, waiting for us to see it and to forge ahead in accordance with its directives. It has a happy ending.

The plan is made up of little things—little todays. It will be revealed to you a little at a time, as much as you can absorb and understand. Don't worry about tomorrow; that's another day. You will know then what to do.

Go within yourself, take faith with you, and ask. Then just listen.

Truth in Advertising

H. LEE JONES

"**P**LAIN FACTS about the polar regions," Vilhjalmur Stefansson, arctic explorer, once told me, "are more fabulous than the popularly accepted fictions. But the public prefers to keep on believing almost everything but the truth.

"Because you're a newspaperman you probably expect me to have something to say about the incredible bleakness of the icebound North, its frigid horrors, the constant dangers lurking in those ghastly, barren wastes. But since those things are fanciful, not actual, I can't say them. The realities are more marvelous than man's misconceptions."

That statement has lingered with me through the years.

Stefansson's was a story of the verdant lushness of those lands, their prodigious productivity in the growing season, their bewildering beauty. These things were more astonishing than any imaginative account of the "terrors" encountered by "the intrepid explorer surrounded by the savage wolf pack" or awaiting starvation or something worse.

"The realities are more marvelous than man's misconceptions."

Stefansson's truism, many of us could agree,

might profitably be taken as a text for advertising
in America. It might be useful—to advertisers, advertising men, advertising mediums—to all engaged
in this big, brash, billion-dollar business. Most important, advertising could thereby perform an even
greater service in the public interest than is cur-
rently the case.

Looking at it retrospectively since World War
I, I find that advertising has made technical advances
in many fields. Radio advertising—then unknown
—has wrought its own miracle in familiarizing the
masses with new material marvels, improved products—countless items, cheap or costly—for which
markets are sought. Advertising has entered an un-
precedented era of expansion. Peacetime production
is creating competitive conditions of the keenest kind
this nation has ever known.

If the art and science of advertising—for it is
both—appear to have been put under indictment
here, let it be understood that "our best friends are
those who tell us of our faults."

Friends offer helpful suggestions if they can.
Carping can't help. Advertising men are themselves
aware of many deficiencies in advertising, from the
solicitation of accounts to innumerable other activities between the conception and the execution of
an advertising program. They realize that many
faults are to be found, from copy department to
printed page, twenty-four-sheets bill board, or radio commercial.

We can here be concerned neither with techniques nor technical matters, however fascinating. We wish to look at advertising purely from a layman's point of view.

A hard-boiled advertising veteran once discovered an associate of mine perusing a book titled "Advertising Principles." "Young man," he said pontifically, "when you've been at it as long as I have, you'll find out this is one racket where there just ain't no principles. Advertising men with principles are all on the path to the poorhouse."

Unprincipled advertising has been the bad apple that, in public opinion, has contaminated the whole advertising barrel. Misleading statements, gross exaggerations, unsupported claims, outright lies, ridiculous and absurd representations, devious devices of a hundred dozen kinds—these have been responsible for impairing and sometimes destroying public faith in advertising and consumer confidence in advertised products.

Many publications decline questionable advertising. Others guarantee that advertising appearing in their pages is reliable: "If our advertisers don't make good—we will!" Wisely managed periodicals are exacting in their ethical requirements. They do not want misrepresentation to kill the goose that produces the golden eggs of advertising revenue.

Advertising is not an entity within itself, separate from and unrelated to other industries. It is not, as is sometimes mistakenly supposed, an activity isolated and apart. It does not "stand on its own legs." Advertising per se is not responsible for itself. It is an integrating function, a force inseparable from other forces that create and sustain it: manufacturing, commerce, industry, distribution—activities beyond number. Upon these forces and the human elements controlling them rests the responsibility for all advertising.

Advertising then is the voice of business. In its voice it reflects the character of the product or service. It reveals as well the character of the persons engaged in our enterprises of production, our vast network of service institutions from the multi-billion-dollar telephone industry to the neighborhood grocery.

Fraudulent advertising—fraudulent in the legal sense—is almost a thing of the past, thanks to influence wielded by honest advertising practitioners themselves, Better Business bureaus, the vigilance of the Federal Trade Commission and postal authorities, the press of America.

Advertising, however—particularly in the more puerile of the pulpfiction publications—still sometimes stoops to false, misleading, and deceptive practices. Even in the "slicks," including high-type, many-million-circulation magazines; in "literary" publications of most excellent editorial standards; on the radio air waves; on television; on outdoor posters and car cards; in the daily press, in trade, technical, industrial, and professional journals; in direct-mail material—in every medium of advertising we may yet discern misrepresentation, extravagance of statement, artifices of many kinds, chicanery—all indicating failure to adhere to the facts.

Since advertising does not "stand on its own legs" and is not responsible for itself it would be unfair to charge publications and other advertising mediums, or the agencies that prepare and place advertising, with the evils, errors, failures, or imperfections of advertising. As well blame the train, the automobile, the streetcar, or the bus for the fact that among the passengers carried are unscrupulous and dishonest persons, thieves, pickpockets, people who still walk in darkness.

The telephone company is not held responsible for the words its wires carry. Nor is "the voice of business"—advertising—to be held accountable for the lapses of those who employ it to carry their messages to the public.

Advertising "sins," like any others, must undergo correction at their source. Invariably that source is human. Yes, "to err is human." But to err purposely, deliberately, and to continue tactics that tend to injure and destroy rather than to benefit and to build—this kind of erring may justly be called into the court of public opinion.

A manufacturer produces a good commodity. He wants to effect distribution as quickly, widely, and economically as possible. He or the firm's advertising manager retains an advertising agency. Because of highly competitive marketing conditions or because of enthusiastic confidence in the product, and sometimes for no reason at all, the agency's "copy" (the words of the advertisement or series of advertisements) contains exaggerated statements, makes claims not justified by the facts.

Before the "copy" appears in print or hits the ether waves it is submitted to the manufacturer, his advertising or sales manager, or others in authority. They cannot escape knowing what it contains. Theirs is the responsibility for any statement relating to the product or the company manufacturing it.

Any assertion that is false, any unwarranted representation, anything violating the principles of good business is open to careful scrutiny by those in the manufacturing firm who know—if anyone does—all about the product. To approve for publication anything patently inaccurate or questionable is to hold expediency to be more desirable than truth.

Advertising associations, agencies, trade publications, organized groups of advertising users, and similar interests have long espoused the cause of "truth in advertising," closer adherence to facts. The cause has made some progress. Immeasurably greater strides must be made if advertising, one of the most potent forces of our time, is to deserve and achieve the magnificent role it could play in human betterment.

Bare conformity by business to established ethics, mere avoidance of dishonesty, cheating, unfairness

—this is not enough to qualify as good business in its deeper implications.

Nor must advertising, a business tool, rest content with tacit compliance with the rules, abstention from overt offenses, rejection of flagrant abuses, eschewing of taboos. Advertising must do more than "get by"; it must "get on."

A group of professional advertising men bent on self-improvement used to gather for a weekly luncheon. There were account executives, copy writers, illustration and layout experts, space buyers, publishers, market-data men, survey and research specialists, merchandising strategists, media masterminds. They held "clinics" on current publication advertising, doing post-mortems on a number of major magazines.

Dissecting a dozen automobile ads, one man deleted identifying trade-marks and slogans and then reproduced on typewritten pages the "copy" or body of the advertisements. Superlatives ran rampant, claims of superiority vied boldly. Each car was the epitome of beauty, safety, comfort, dependability, economy in operation; each was the quintessence of all a motorcar could be. Only two men were able to recognize what makes of cars were described; even they failed to distinguish more than a few.

Marked success often attends advertising that plainly, simply, honestly (and hence convincingly) states the literal truth, even—in store copy—to the point of admitting such facts as "shopworn," "out of style," "poor quality," "substandard grade," "rejects," "imitation." Sincerity is a contagious thing conveying itself inevitably to reader and listener.

No amount of advertising can endow a product or service with merits that are not inherent in it.

Successful advertising, say experts, must do four things: arrest attention, arouse interest, create desire, induce action. None of these requirements is dependent on a departure from honest methods, factual representations.

Confidence in the quality of the thing advertised does not call for overstatement. A real-estate concern advertising a new and superior subdivision ran a full-page newspaper advertisement headed: "Don't Look at Lovato Heights until You've Seen Everything Else in Town!" The firm's salesmen were instructed to offer to take prospects to view all the other home-building sections first. This was no mere gesture of generosity. If potential buyers saw all the less desirable offerings, that fact itself would give Lovato Heights the decisive advantage. The subdivision in question became and remains today the community's finest.

In part advertising has gradually groped its way from false assertion to factual statement. For that advance it deserves approbation, encouragement.

Beyond fact telling advertising may enhance its value by seeking something more than mere accord with material truth. It cannot come fully into its own until it transcends that limitation. By enlarging its vision to encompass something more significant than "salesmanship in print," advertising can train its sights upward—toward spiritual Truth.

Already many national manufacturers and service institutions devote their printed messages neither to product promotion nor service selling except in a most minor or incidental manner. Subscribing to the truth contained in Stefansson's statement, their advertising has approximated an unselfish public service. It is serving to focus the attention of millions on the truth that "the realities are more marvelous than man's misconceptions." These advertising pioneers— ostensibly giving more than they receive—are reaping an incalculable harvest of public confidence and good will.

Advertising need not abandon its essential function as a "mover of goods." As such it has brought success to a host of business enterprises—and public benefits as well.

In dedicating itself to a still larger purpose, advertising—most articulate of all arts—may become one of mankind's "prime movers" toward all that is good "in spirit and truth."

Are You Serving Your Troubles?

HAROLD S. KAHM

I T WAS A WARM spring day in New York, one of those perfect days when the very exhaust fumes of the Fifth Avenue busses seem to smell like perfume. It was a day for happiness, for the heart is meant to sing in perfect weather. But no one could have convinced me that it was a nice day. To me it was a dark, horrid day because I was worried about my income, and my prayers had not been answered.

It takes a special kind of temperament to enable a man to laugh and be gay when he is behind in his room rent and doesn't know where his next meal is coming from. Or it takes faith in the good. I wanted to have faith and I told myself I did have it, but judging from the results apparent so far, it didn't seem to be of a very good quality, because my affairs seemed to be growing steadily worse.

It was twelve o'clock noon, and I found myself gazing wistfully through the huge plate-glass window of a big Broadway restaurant. A large sign read, "Blue Plate Special, 65¢." I had just forty cents in my pocket. I looked around for a good place to get a sandwich and a cup of coffee.

As a matter of fact, I was pretty mad at God.

I had fairly prayed my head off these last weeks, but that didn't prevent the stories and articles I had sent out to various magazines from coming right back and slapping me in the face. The pain in my heart was a physical pain, or that is what it felt like at least. Discouragement and despair are not really sharp; they are dull, like rusty knives, and they twist into your soul.

How silly it seemed to me to pray to an invisible God to take a direct hand in my material welfare! God, I told myself, if there was a God, was probably laughing at me. I must have been a sorry sight at that; my pants had not been pressed in two weeks. I had not wanted to waste the money.

I had been trying halfheartedly to get a job, but jobs were scarce. I knew almost no one in New York, and the marvel is that I didn't throw myself off the Brooklyn Bridge.

The worst hurt of all, I think, was the thought that my religion had failed me.

I was a brand-new student of Truth at the time and I had been sure I had finally found the answer to all problems. God was within me, and He would grant every good wish. Oh, yeah? That was my reaction to the whole thing in the midst of this blast of trouble. I felt that God had let me down hard.

I walked down Broadway, after I had had my meager lunch, wondering if I was going to have an attack of indigestion. My stomach felt queasy, for my whole nervous system was strained to the breaking point. What was I going to do? Where could I turn? Where would the money come from for my sustenance? How could I pay my rent? I could give you a complete list of my troubled thoughts but it would be too depressing.

I found myself presently walking along 32d Street and soon I stopped before the building that housed the modest offices of a magazine to which I had recently sent a manuscript. The manuscript had not yet been returned. Perhaps—yes, there was just a chance it might have been accepted. Maybe I could go into that building and come out with a check!

"I'd like to see the editor," I told the girl at the switchboard. "My name is Harold Kahm."

"Miss Brown is busy just now," said the girl pleasantly, "but she'll be through in a few minutes if you care to wait."

Well, that was something. In many editorial offices in New York you had to have what amounted to a passport from Washington to see an editor if you were a nobody like myself.

Miss Brown proved to be a charming woman of about thirty. She smiled me into a seat. "Oh, yes, that little article of yours," she said. "I think we may be able to use it in a later issue."

I could scarcely believe my ears. At last I had had something accepted for a change! "Do you suppose," I faltered, "I could have a check for it now?"

"I wish I could do that," replied Miss Brown, "but we pay only on publication. It's a very strict company rule, but I'll try to use your piece as soon as possible—perhaps even next month."

There was something about Miss Brown . . . I found myself telling her all my troubles, and she listened with sympathy, as if all she had to do in this world was to listen to my troubles. I even told her how God had failed me. I told her everything—and it was quite a relief to get it off my chest.

"You know," she said thoughtfully, "I think I know what your real trouble is. You're serving the wrong master."

"What do you mean?"

"Jesus made it very clear that no man can serve two masters," she said. "You can't serve God and serve another master at the same time. You're serving your troubles. You think about them when you should be thinking about God. You put God on one side and your troubles on the other and you turn all of your real attention to those troubles.

"You don't believe in God half as much as you do in the immediate fact of your difficulties. Isn't that true?"

I stared at her in stunned silence. If she had suddenly hit me over the head with her typewriter, I don't think I could have been more shocked, for there was the ring of absolute conviction in her accusation.

"You see," she smiled, "I've been a Truth student

for several years and I've discovered many things. I
used to do the very same thing you're doing now.
I placed my real faith in my difficulties. When I
prayed, what I really believed in was those obstacles,
and God only answers prayer when a person believes
his prayer will be answered—really believes completely and absolutely deep in his innermost being.
But you can't possibly have faith in God and faith
in trouble at the same time. You must take your
choice."

I think now that this was one of the most important days of my life, for it was the first time
anyone had made me realize with the utmost clarity
where I had been making my mistake.

I know many others are making that same error
today. In their experience I see a vivid reflection
of my own early misunderstanding. A woman will
write to me telling me her troubles in great detail.
She is wholly submerged in them; they are with
her day and night usurping her consciousness, and
she complains that she has prayed endlessly for relief but that God has not responded.

Her case is readily explained. Jesus said, "Whatsoever ye shall ask in prayer, believing, ye shall receive." She does not believe that her prayers will
be answered; she believes in her troubles and their
power to oppose her. Jesus said, "No man can
serve two masters." She serves her obstacles by accepting them and believing in them.

When I walked out of Miss Brown's office on

that memorable day, I felt as if a great weight had been lifted from my heart. The veil had been removed from my eyes. Now I saw the beauty of the spring day and its wonderful promise of the summer to come. With terrible clarity, I realized that I had been worshiping evil instead of good. I had worshiped it as one should worship only God, with complete and absolute acceptance.

Of what possible use could it be to think about my troubles when only God had the power to change my circumstances? "I can of myself do nothing."

There was a new spring in my step as I walked toward the subway, and a new resolution in my heart. Henceforward, I would think only of God and not of my difficulties. Thinking about my troubles would only make them worse; thinking about God and accepting Him utterly would change everything.

Like some kindly magic this resolution immediately altered my whole mood. I had flung off my sense of oppression and discouragement and turned my troubles over to God. They were His responsibility now, not mine! He, not I, would show me the way out. Stubbornly, I shut my eyes to my circumstances.

Then I examined the extent of my faith. What did I actually believe? What could I pray for specifically that I had the absolute conviction I would receive? Well, for one thing. I knew perfectly well in my heart that I would not starve. That I could

most emphatically believe, even though I could
not see the means of my sustenance in prospect. I
also could wholly believe that I would not have to
sleep in the street and I also could believe thoroughly
that I would not spend the rest of my life in poverty.

Therefore, I could now pray with perfect confidence and ask for my daily bread, for shelter, for
prosperity. As long as I believed, no power on earth
could keep these things from me! This was Jesus'
promise.

For days I had been unable to write; my energy
had flagged, and my inspiration was absent. All
my talents had been devoted to thinking how miserable and hopeless was my situation. Now there was
a change. Once again I felt lighthearted. I was no
longer trying to boss my own affairs; God was doing
that now, because I had stopped. What God sent, I
would accept. I would simply follow my heart.

My fingers flew over the typewriter when I returned to my little room. I hoped that the next mail
would bring me a check, but I resolved that no
matter what happened I would not falter in my
determination to trust God and to leave to Him
the manner in which I should have my prayer answered.

Strangely enough, I felt relieved the next morning when I had spent my last dime for breakfast.
Now I knew that God would act! Never before or
since has my faith been stronger. I was utterly helpless. Of myself I could do nothing. I recognized

this fact with all the fervor of my being, and I looked to God as a little child looks to his father.

When the mail came at 10 o'clock there was no check, but there was something else: a letter from an editor giving me an assignment for an article. At noon, when I began to think that I might have to pawn my signet ring, there was a knock on my door. A friend of mine, who had been out of town, had come over to invite me to lunch. And what a lunch it was! Six courses at a wonderful little Italian restaurant in the Village.

"How are you making out?" my friend wanted to know as we relaxed after dinner. I told him the truth. He insisted (without much resistance on my part!) on lending me twenty-five dollars. There was no hurry about paying it back, he assured me. He had a good job, and if I didn't repay the loan in five years it was O. K. with him.

Within three days I received a check for fifteen dollars and two days later another one for eight dollars. I was practically a millionaire! Now my room rent was paid up, my shoes were shined, my clothes were pressed, my stomach was too full for my own good. I was on top of the world. How I regretted those dark days when I had wasted my energy serving my troubles instead of God.

It was with a little shock of surprise that I realized that even in my darkest hours I had not actually gone hungry or been without any other of the necessities of life. It was the thought of being without them that had pained me, not the actuality.

How different my life was from then on. Sometimes when the shadow of evil confronted me it was something of a struggle not to give in to my old errors of thinking, but generally I was successful in combatting them. I could not and would not serve two masters. I had only one master, God.

I know that many other Truth students wonder why their prayers do not seem to be answered and I would like them to benefit from my experience. When you seem to be in trouble, ask yourself whether you are accepting those troubles, recognizing and believing in them. If you have been making that mistake it is time for you to say, "Get thee behind me, Satan!" and turn your attention solely to God. For it is as true as the rising and setting of the sun that no man can serve two masters and that "whatsoever ye shall ask in prayer, *believing,* ye shall receive."

Do you believe in your troubles—or in God? I have engraved this question on my heart, and it has never failed to turn my thinking from the bad to perfect good. If you ask it of yourself with absolute honesty, you will find the major answer to the question whether God will answer your prayers.

Any Job You Want

GARDNER HUNTING

Y OU can have any job you want. You do not
believe that, do you? That is why you do
not get the job you want now; you do not
believe you can get it.

Did you ever hear Mark Twain's advice to the
young seeker after a job? He said something like
this: "Pick out the man you want to work for, and
then go and work for him. Tell him you are going
to work for him for nothing till he decides you are
worth something, and how much." That seems an
absurd piece of advice. But it will certainly work if
you really put it into practice. Now, think a moment
with me.

If you get a job—any sort of a job—what will
your employer pay you for? For the work you do,
of course. Will he pay you in advance? He will not.
He will pay you after you have worked a month, a
week, a day. How much will he pay you? What you
earn, of course. Will he pay you more than you are
worth—even if he has agreed to? He will not. If
you do not measure up to specifications, he will get
out of his agreement in one way or another. He will
discharge you, or if he has made a contract with you,
he will break it or make you break it, or he will

make your situation intolerable, or buy you off. He will certainly not pay you for something you do not give him.

In the business world there is a saying that you cannot get something for nothing. You cannot. This means that you cannot get salary or wages for something you do not do. Do you think you see men getting paid for something they are not delivering? Watch them. Watch the loafers and the quitters and the "soldiers."

But there is a deeper thing under this fact and these appearances than people commonly think. It is this: Justice! Justice does work in the affairs of men, whether they recognize it or not. You do not believe it? Study it. Men do get what they want—what they really want. You can get what you really want, as we have said—and you will get it, whether you know it or not!

"But," you say, "just as good men have failed of their aim as have succeeded." So? What does it mean to be "good"? Goodness, in the ordinary sense, has nothing to do with the matter; otherwise we could not understand the situation at all. People who try to explain success or failure on the ground of goodness never do understand it. "Goodness" or "badness" in the ordinary moral sense is not the reason. Law is the reason for everything.

Real virtue consists in keeping in harmony with the law—or trying to. Goodness in this sense is always rewarded, and badness in the same sense is always punished. That is, the law works for those who keep it and works against those who go against it. I do not dare to set any limits. I do not believe there are any limits. It does not make the least difference in the world whether we know the law or not—it works. "Ignorance of the law is no excuse." And you cannot blame some far-off God for your actions, or for anything that happens to you, or for your knowing the law or not knowing it. It is up to you!

Does that frighten you? Or if you believed it, would it frighten you? Instead of frightening you it should encourage you, inspire you, stir you up to your highest ambition, fill you with your highest hope, assure you of realization of your highest desire, make you certain of success, and happy beyond your dreams! Because you cannot lose!

Now, let us see. We have made some pretty rash statements, have we not? From the ordinary, unbelieving standpoint, yes. But it is not bumptiousness to state law, nor modesty to understate it. What have we said? You can have anything you really want. Well, you can; the thing you want is among the possibilities for you or you would not want it. Desire is implanted in you by a power that intends you to have what that desire calls for. You have no desires that this power has not given you. Desire was meant to be fulfilled, consuming, supreme desire, not the piddling little wishes that do not even last over night or past mealtime. Your real desire becomes the great purpose of your life; and it matters not what the purpose is, you are going to get a reward commensurate with your singleheartedness. Besides, your desire is implanted in you by this power we are talking about.

This power will grant the desire. This power is the only power there is in the universe. It is the power for which another name is God. God is the only power you will ever know; the only power you will ever get a job from; the only power you will ever work for; and the only power that will ever pay you. You may think you ask some man or woman for a job, but you do not really. You "ask" the universal law for that job. And because the universal law (God) has put the desire for that job in you, you will get it. And because that same universal law is the paymaster you will get paid for it, and no man or woman on earth can prevent it. You are working for God, not man. God is the one to whom you go for your job, for whom you labor, from whom you receive your reward. You cannot help it; that is the way it is. It is so, whether you believe it or not, whether you know it or not, whether you like it or not!

But you remind me that I have said that all desire comes from God. It may be well enough to think that the desire to work comes from the one power, but does the desire of the sitter to sit come also from the Supreme Being? Why, certainly! In Him I live, and move and have my being; I have nothing without Him. Yes, even my desire to sit! But who is God? Why, God is my being. God is my life, my strength, my intelligence, my mind. Now turn the statement around. My being is God, my life is God, my intelligence is God, my mind is God. Do you pretend to say that you have a desire independent of your mind? Hardly. Well, that is the answer.

The answer is that God, instead of being something outside of you, is within you, controlling all your affairs through you. I believe that you have only to realize that overwhelming conception in order to have God come forth visibly into your affairs, whatever they are, whoever you are, wherever you are, whatever your circumstances appear to be. You are an individual expression of God. You create what you choose. How? First by thinking it. That is the only way anything is created—by thought. If you think that things are created by hammer and nails or power shovels or dynamos or lathes or trowels or giant power or printing presses or congresses or kings, you have never thought even so far back as the drafting table or the blue pencil!

Things are created by thought in the mind—yes, by your thought and in your mind. When you begin to realize that, you will begin to work for the God who is universal Mind, in you and in me and in everybody else, and in everything in the universe. You will realize that you cannot fail to do what you really want to do and have what you really want to have.

How shall you begin? By going after that first
job with an idea in your mind just the reverse of
what you have been trying to hold there. Think not
about what you are going to get but about what you
can give. Ask for opportunity to give and give with
all your heart all you have got, knowing that you
cannot fail to get what your desire calls for. You
cannot fail to get back what you give out. For who
are you? You are the expression of God in your
individuality. Think of that. In Him you live and
move and have your being. You are one with God,
the supreme power in the universe. You are one with
supreme universal Mind. And universal Mind creates
what it wants to create. In other words, it gives out
what it wants to see manifested. Think of it, Think!
You! Not somebody else—you! You cannot fail!

"Read this book
one and one.
You will master
what you work."

Publisher's Announcement

Prayer in the Market Place is published by the Unity School of Christianity, an independent educational institution devoted to teaching the principles of Christianity and the application of these principles to everyday life and affairs. In addition to *Prayer in the Market Place,* Unity School publishes:

These books cover so many subjects of general and vital interest that among them you are sure to find one that meets a need of your own or that of a friend. Beautifully bound, these lovely Unity books are priced at $2 each unless otherwise indicated.

UNITY SCHOOL OF CHRISTIANITY
Lee's Summit, Missouri

PRINTED U.S.A.   5F-4M-2-59